C-244   CAREER EXAMINATION SERIES

This is your
PASSBOOK for...

Elevator Inspector

Test Preparation Study Guide
Questions & Answers

COPYRIGHT NOTICE

This book is SOLELY intended for, is sold ONLY to, and its use is RESTRICTED to individual, bona fide applicants or candidates who qualify by virtue of having seriously filed applications for appropriate license, certificate, professional and/or promotional advancement, higher school matriculation, scholarship, or other legitimate requirements of education and/or governmental authorities.

This book is NOT intended for use, class instruction, tutoring, training, duplication, copying, reprinting, excerption, or adaptation, etc., by:

1) Other publishers
2) Proprietors and/or Instructors of "Coaching" and/or Preparatory Courses
3) Personnel and/or Training Divisions of commercial, industrial, and governmental organizations
4) Schools, colleges, or universities and/or their departments and staffs, including teachers and other personnel
5) Testing Agencies or Bureaus
6) Study groups which seek by the purchase of a single volume to copy and/or duplicate and/or adapt this material for use by the group as a whole without having purchased individual volumes for each of the members of the group
7) Et al.

Such persons would be in violation of appropriate Federal and State statutes.

PROVISION OF LICENSING AGREEMENTS – Recognized educational, commercial, industrial, and governmental institutions and organizations, and others legitimately engaged in educational pursuits, including training, testing, and measurement activities, may address request for a licensing agreement to the copyright owners, who will determine whether, and under what conditions, including fees and charges, the materials in this book may be used them. In other words, a licensing facility exists for the legitimate use of the material in this book on other than an individual basis. However, it is asseverated and affirmed here that the material in this book CANNOT be used without the receipt of the express permission of such a licensing agreement from the Publishers. Inquiries re licensing should be addressed to the company, attention rights and permissions department.

All rights reserved, including the right of reproduction in whole or in part, in any form or by any means, electronic or mechanical, including photocopying, recording, or by any information storage and retrieval system, without permission in writing from the Publisher.

Copyright © 2024 by
National Learning Corporation

212 Michael Drive, Syosset, NY 11791
(516) 921-8888 • www.passbooks.com
E-mail: info@passbooks.com

PASSBOOK® SERIES

THE *PASSBOOK® SERIES* has been created to prepare applicants and candidates for the ultimate academic battlefield – the examination room.

At some time in our lives, each and every one of us may be required to take an examination – for validation, matriculation, admission, qualification, registration, certification, or licensure.

Based on the assumption that every applicant or candidate has met the basic formal educational standards, has taken the required number of courses, and read the necessary texts, the *PASSBOOK® SERIES* furnishes the one special preparation which may assure passing with confidence, instead of failing with insecurity. Examination questions – together with answers – are furnished as the basic vehicle for study so that the mysteries of the examination and its compounding difficulties may be eliminated or diminished by a sure method.

This book is meant to help you pass your examination provided that you qualify and are serious in your objective.

The entire field is reviewed through the huge store of content information which is succinctly presented through a provocative and challenging approach – the question-and-answer method.

A climate of success is established by furnishing the correct answers at the end of each test.

You soon learn to recognize types of questions, forms of questions, and patterns of questioning. You may even begin to anticipate expected outcomes.

You perceive that many questions are repeated or adapted so that you can gain acute insights, which may enable you to score many sure points.

You learn how to confront new questions, or types of questions, and to attack them confidently and work out the correct answers.

You note objectives and emphases, and recognize pitfalls and dangers, so that you may make positive educational adjustments.

Moreover, you are kept fully informed in relation to new concepts, methods, practices, and directions in the field.

You discover that you are actually taking the examination all the time: you are preparing for the examination by "taking" an examination, not by reading extraneous and/or supererogatory textbooks.

In short, this PASSBOOK®, used directedly, should be an important factor in helping you to pass your test.

ELEVATOR INSPECTOR

DUTIES:
Elevator Inspectors , under general supervision, perform technical work in the inspection of the construction, alteration, capacity and safety of equipment and devices, including passenger, freight and sidewalk elevators, escalators, dumb-waiters, wheelchair lifts, conveyors, personal hoists and amusement devices, for compliance with the provisions of the building code and with pertinent laws and regulations; within an assigned district, they periodically and in response to complaints about hazardous conditions, inspect the condition and functioning of all parts of elevators, including shafts, ropes, cables, rails, beams, switches, doors, gears, motors, controllers, pumps, governors, safeties, automatic stops and other appunenances; witness mandatory tests of safety devices and safety tests on all high speed elevators; inspect the installation and alteration of such equipment and devices to determine if the work is performed in a workmanlike manner and in compliance with approved plans and specifications and witness final testing of new equipment; issue notices of violation, or if condition of equipment is deemed dangerous, may order discontinuation of the elevator service; make re-inspections of pending violations and recommend appropriate action; make survey changes of occupancy where it pertains to safety features of the elevators; perform audit inspections to verify the work being performed or certified by outside elevator agencies; prepare related reports; may operate a motor vehicle in the performance of assigned duties; may supervise and train Apprentice Inspectors; may assist an Associate Inspector; perform related work.

SCOPE OF THE EXAMINATION
The multiple choice test may include questions on elevators, escalators and other lifting and moving devices (i.e., amusement rides, wheelchair lifts, dumbwaiters, etc.), their functions and applicable code requirements and laws; electrical, mechanical, hydraulic principles, and safety practices as applied to elevators, escalators,and other lifting and moving devices; job-related numeric calculations; written expression; reading comprehension; the ability to apply rules to specific problems to come up with logical answers; the ability to think of possible reasons why things go together based on separate pieces of information; and other related areas.

HOW TO TAKE A TEST

I. YOU MUST PASS AN EXAMINATION

A. WHAT EVERY CANDIDATE SHOULD KNOW

Examination applicants often ask us for help in preparing for the written test. What can I study in advance? What kinds of questions will be asked? How will the test be given? How will the papers be graded?

As an applicant for a civil service examination, you may be wondering about some of these things. Our purpose here is to suggest effective methods of advance study and to describe civil service examinations.

Your chances for success on this examination can be increased if you know how to prepare. Those "pre-examination jitters" can be reduced if you know what to expect. You can even experience an adventure in good citizenship if you know why civil service exams are given.

B. WHY ARE CIVIL SERVICE EXAMINATIONS GIVEN?

Civil service examinations are important to you in two ways. As a citizen, you want public jobs filled by employees who know how to do their work. As a job seeker, you want a fair chance to compete for that job on an equal footing with other candidates. The best-known means of accomplishing this two-fold goal is the competitive examination.

Exams are widely publicized throughout the nation. They may be administered for jobs in federal, state, city, municipal, town or village governments or agencies.

Any citizen may apply, with some limitations, such as the age or residence of applicants. Your experience and education may be reviewed to see whether you meet the requirements for the particular examination. When these requirements exist, they are reasonable and applied consistently to all applicants. Thus, a competitive examination may cause you some uneasiness now, but it is your privilege and safeguard.

C. HOW ARE CIVIL SERVICE EXAMS DEVELOPED?

Examinations are carefully written by trained technicians who are specialists in the field known as "psychological measurement," in consultation with recognized authorities in the field of work that the test will cover. These experts recommend the subject matter areas or skills to be tested; only those knowledges or skills important to your success on the job are included. The most reliable books and source materials available are used as references. Together, the experts and technicians judge the difficulty level of the questions.

Test technicians know how to phrase questions so that the problem is clearly stated. Their ethics do not permit "trick" or "catch" questions. Questions may have been tried out on sample groups, or subjected to statistical analysis, to determine their usefulness.

Written tests are often used in combination with performance tests, ratings of training and experience, and oral interviews. All of these measures combine to form the best-known means of finding the right person for the right job.

II. HOW TO PASS THE WRITTEN TEST

A. NATURE OF THE EXAMINATION

To prepare intelligently for civil service examinations, you should know how they differ from school examinations you have taken. In school you were assigned certain definite pages to read or subjects to cover. The examination questions were quite detailed and usually emphasized memory. Civil service exams, on the other hand, try to discover your present ability to perform the duties of a position, plus your potentiality to learn these duties. In other words, a civil service exam attempts to predict how successful you will be. Questions cover such a broad area that they cannot be as minute and detailed as school exam questions.

In the public service similar kinds of work, or positions, are grouped together in one "class." This process is known as *position-classification*. All the positions in a class are paid according to the salary range for that class. One class title covers all of these positions, and they are all tested by the same examination.

B. FOUR BASIC STEPS

1) Study the announcement

How, then, can you know what subjects to study? Our best answer is: "Learn as much as possible about the class of positions for which you've applied." The exam will test the knowledge, skills and abilities needed to do the work.

Your most valuable source of information about the position you want is the official exam announcement. This announcement lists the training and experience qualifications. Check these standards and apply only if you come reasonably close to meeting them.

The brief description of the position in the examination announcement offers some clues to the subjects which will be tested. Think about the job itself. Review the duties in your mind. Can you perform them, or are there some in which you are rusty? Fill in the blank spots in your preparation.

Many jurisdictions preview the written test in the exam announcement by including a section called "Knowledge and Abilities Required," "Scope of the Examination," or some similar heading. Here you will find out specifically what fields will be tested.

2) Review your own background

Once you learn in general what the position is all about, and what you need to know to do the work, ask yourself which subjects you already know fairly well and which need improvement. You may wonder whether to concentrate on improving your strong areas or on building some background in your fields of weakness. When the announcement has specified "some knowledge" or "considerable knowledge," or has used adjectives like "beginning principles of…" or "advanced … methods," you can get a clue as to the number and difficulty of questions to be asked in any given field. More questions, and hence broader coverage, would be included for those subjects which are more important in the work. Now weigh your strengths and weaknesses against the job requirements and prepare accordingly.

3) Determine the level of the position

Another way to tell how intensively you should prepare is to understand the level of the job for which you are applying. Is it the entering level? In other words, is this the position in which beginners in a field of work are hired? Or is it an intermediate or advanced level? Sometimes this is indicated by such words as "Junior" or "Senior" in the class title. Other jurisdictions use Roman numerals to designate the level – Clerk I, Clerk II, for example. The word "Supervisor" sometimes appears in the title. If the level is not indicated by the title, check the description of duties. Will you be working under very close supervision, or will you have responsibility for independent decisions in this work?

4) Choose appropriate study materials

Now that you know the subjects to be examined and the relative amount of each subject to be covered, you can choose suitable study materials. For beginning level jobs, or even advanced ones, if you have a pronounced weakness in some aspect of your training, read a modern, standard textbook in that field. Be sure it is up to date and has general coverage. Such books are normally available at your library, and the librarian will be glad to help you locate one. For entry-level positions, questions of appropriate difficulty are chosen – neither highly advanced questions, nor those too simple. Such questions require careful thought but not advanced training.

If the position for which you are applying is technical or advanced, you will read more advanced, specialized material. If you are already familiar with the basic principles of your field, elementary textbooks would waste your time. Concentrate on advanced textbooks and technical periodicals. Think through the concepts and review difficult problems in your field.

These are all general sources. You can get more ideas on your own initiative, following these leads. For example, training manuals and publications of the government agency which employs workers in your field can be useful, particularly for technical and professional positions. A letter or visit to the government department involved may result in more specific study suggestions, and certainly will provide you with a more definite idea of the exact nature of the position you are seeking.

III. KINDS OF TESTS

Tests are used for purposes other than measuring knowledge and ability to perform specified duties. For some positions, it is equally important to test ability to make adjustments to new situations or to profit from training. In others, basic mental abilities not dependent on information are essential. Questions which test these things may not appear as pertinent to the duties of the position as those which test for knowledge and information. Yet they are often highly important parts of a fair examination. For very general questions, it is almost impossible to help you direct your study efforts. What we can do is to point out some of the more common of these general abilities needed in public service positions and describe some typical questions.

1) General information

Broad, general information has been found useful for predicting job success in some kinds of work. This is tested in a variety of ways, from vocabulary lists to questions about current events. Basic background in some field of work, such as sociology or economics, may be sampled in a group of questions. Often these are principles which have become familiar to most persons through exposure rather than through formal training. It is difficult to advise you how to study for these questions; being alert to the world around you is our best suggestion.

2) Verbal ability

An example of an ability needed in many positions is verbal or language ability. Verbal ability is, in brief, the ability to use and understand words. Vocabulary and grammar tests are typical measures of this ability. Reading comprehension or paragraph interpretation questions are common in many kinds of civil service tests. You are given a paragraph of written material and asked to find its central meaning.

3) Numerical ability

Number skills can be tested by the familiar arithmetic problem, by checking paired lists of numbers to see which are alike and which are different, or by interpreting charts and graphs. In the latter test, a graph may be printed in the test booklet which you are asked to use as the basis for answering questions.

4) Observation

A popular test for law-enforcement positions is the observation test. A picture is shown to you for several minutes, then taken away. Questions about the picture test your ability to observe both details and larger elements.

5) Following directions

In many positions in the public service, the employee must be able to carry out written instructions dependably and accurately. You may be given a chart with several columns, each column listing a variety of information. The questions require you to carry out directions involving the information given in the chart.

6) Skills and aptitudes

Performance tests effectively measure some manual skills and aptitudes. When the skill is one in which you are trained, such as typing or shorthand, you can practice. These tests are often very much like those given in business school or high school courses. For many of the other skills and aptitudes, however, no short-time preparation can be made. Skills and abilities natural to you or that you have developed throughout your lifetime are being tested.

Many of the general questions just described provide all the data needed to answer the questions and ask you to use your reasoning ability to find the answers. Your best preparation for these tests, as well as for tests of facts and ideas, is to be at your physical and mental best. You, no doubt, have your own methods of getting into an exam-taking mood and keeping "in shape." The next section lists some ideas on this subject.

IV. KINDS OF QUESTIONS

Only rarely is the "essay" question, which you answer in narrative form, used in civil service tests. Civil service tests are usually of the short-answer type. Full instructions for answering these questions will be given to you at the examination. But in case this is your first experience with short-answer questions and separate answer sheets, here is what you need to know:

1) **Multiple-choice Questions**

Most popular of the short-answer questions is the "multiple choice" or "best answer" question. It can be used, for example, to test for factual knowledge, ability to solve problems or judgment in meeting situations found at work.

A multiple-choice question is normally one of three types—
- It can begin with an incomplete statement followed by several possible endings. You are to find the one ending which *best* completes the statement, although some of the others may not be entirely wrong.
- It can also be a complete statement in the form of a question which is answered by choosing one of the statements listed.

- It can be in the form of a problem – again you select the best answer.

Here is an example of a multiple-choice question with a discussion which should give you some clues as to the method for choosing the right answer:

When an employee has a complaint about his assignment, the action which will *best* help him overcome his difficulty is to
    A. discuss his difficulty with his coworkers
    B. take the problem to the head of the organization
    C. take the problem to the person who gave him the assignment
    D. say nothing to anyone about his complaint

In answering this question, you should study each of the choices to find which is best. Consider choice "A" – Certainly an employee may discuss his complaint with fellow employees, but no change or improvement can result, and the complaint remains unresolved. Choice "B" is a poor choice since the head of the organization probably does not know what assignment you have been given, and taking your problem to him is known as "going over the head" of the supervisor. The supervisor, or person who made the assignment, is the person who can clarify it or correct any injustice. Choice "C" is, therefore, correct. To say nothing, as in choice "D," is unwise. Supervisors have and interest in knowing the problems employees are facing, and the employee is seeking a solution to his problem.

2) True/False Questions

The "true/false" or "right/wrong" form of question is sometimes used. Here a complete statement is given. Your job is to decide whether the statement is right or wrong.

SAMPLE: A roaming cell-phone call to a nearby city costs less than a non-roaming call to a distant city.

This statement is wrong, or false, since roaming calls are more expensive.

This is not a complete list of all possible question forms, although most of the others are variations of these common types. You will always get complete directions for answering questions. Be sure you understand *how* to mark your answers – ask questions until you do.

V. RECORDING YOUR ANSWERS

Computer terminals are used more and more today for many different kinds of exams.
For an examination with very few applicants, you may be told to record your answers in the test booklet itself. Separate answer sheets are much more common. If this separate answer sheet is to be scored by machine – and this is often the case – it is highly important that you mark your answers correctly in order to get credit.

An electronic scoring machine is often used in civil service offices because of the speed with which papers can be scored. Machine-scored answer sheets must be marked with a pencil, which will be given to you. This pencil has a high graphite content which responds to the electronic scoring machine. As a matter of fact, stray dots may register as answers, so do not let your pencil rest on the answer sheet while you are pondering the correct answer. Also, if your pencil lead breaks or is otherwise defective, ask for another.

Since the answer sheet will be dropped in a slot in the scoring machine, be careful not to bend the corners or get the paper crumpled.

The answer sheet normally has five vertical columns of numbers, with 30 numbers to a column. These numbers correspond to the question numbers in your test booklet. After each number, going across the page are four or five pairs of dotted lines. These short dotted lines have small letters or numbers above them. The first two pairs may also have a "T" or "F" above the letters. This indicates that the first two pairs only are to be used if the questions are of the true-false type. If the questions are multiple choice, disregard the "T" and "F" and pay attention only to the small letters or numbers.

Answer your questions in the manner of the sample that follows:

32. The largest city in the United States is
    A. Washington, D.C.
    B. New York City
    C. Chicago
    D. Detroit
    E. San Francisco

1) Choose the answer you think is best. (New York City is the largest, so "B" is correct.)
2) Find the row of dotted lines numbered the same as the question you are answering. (Find row number 32)
3) Find the pair of dotted lines corresponding to the answer. (Find the pair of lines under the mark "B.")
4) Make a solid black mark between the dotted lines.

VI. BEFORE THE TEST

Common sense will help you find procedures to follow to get ready for an examination. Too many of us, however, overlook these sensible measures. Indeed, nervousness and fatigue have been found to be the most serious reasons why applicants fail to do their best on civil service tests. Here is a list of reminders:

- Begin your preparation early – Don't wait until the last minute to go scurrying around for books and materials or to find out what the position is all about.
- Prepare continuously – An hour a night for a week is better than an all-night cram session. This has been definitely established. What is more, a night a week for a month will return better dividends than crowding your study into a shorter period of time.
- Locate the place of the exam – You have been sent a notice telling you when and where to report for the examination. If the location is in a different town or otherwise unfamiliar to you, it would be well to inquire the best route and learn something about the building.
- Relax the night before the test – Allow your mind to rest. Do not study at all that night. Plan some mild recreation or diversion; then go to bed early and get a good night's sleep.
- Get up early enough to make a leisurely trip to the place for the test – This way unforeseen events, traffic snarls, unfamiliar buildings, etc. will not upset you.
- Dress comfortably – A written test is not a fashion show. You will be known by number and not by name, so wear something comfortable.

- Leave excess paraphernalia at home – Shopping bags and odd bundles will get in your way. You need bring only the items mentioned in the official notice you received; usually everything you need is provided. Do not bring reference books to the exam. They will only confuse those last minutes and be taken away from you when in the test room.
- Arrive somewhat ahead of time – If because of transportation schedules you must get there very early, bring a newspaper or magazine to take your mind off yourself while waiting.
- Locate the examination room – When you have found the proper room, you will be directed to the seat or part of the room where you will sit. Sometimes you are given a sheet of instructions to read while you are waiting. Do not fill out any forms until you are told to do so; just read them and be prepared.
- Relax and prepare to listen to the instructions
- If you have any physical problem that may keep you from doing your best, be sure to tell the test administrator. If you are sick or in poor health, you really cannot do your best on the exam. You can come back and take the test some other time.

VII. AT THE TEST

The day of the test is here and you have the test booklet in your hand. The temptation to get going is very strong. Caution! There is more to success than knowing the right answers. You must know how to identify your papers and understand variations in the type of short-answer question used in this particular examination. Follow these suggestions for maximum results from your efforts:

1) Cooperate with the monitor

The test administrator has a duty to create a situation in which you can be as much at ease as possible. He will give instructions, tell you when to begin, check to see that you are marking your answer sheet correctly, and so on. He is not there to guard you, although he will see that your competitors do not take unfair advantage. He wants to help you do your best.

2) Listen to all instructions

Don't jump the gun! Wait until you understand all directions. In most civil service tests you get more time than you need to answer the questions. So don't be in a hurry. Read each word of instructions until you clearly understand the meaning. Study the examples, listen to all announcements and follow directions. Ask questions if you do not understand what to do.

3) Identify your papers

Civil service exams are usually identified by number only. You will be assigned a number; you must not put your name on your test papers. Be sure to copy your number correctly. Since more than one exam may be given, copy your exact examination title.

4) Plan your time

Unless you are told that a test is a "speed" or "rate of work" test, speed itself is usually not important. Time enough to answer all the questions will be provided, but this does not mean that you have all day. An overall time limit has been set. Divide the total time (in minutes) by the number of questions to determine the approximate time you have for each question.

5) Do not linger over difficult questions

If you come across a difficult question, mark it with a paper clip (useful to have along) and come back to it when you have been through the booklet. One caution if you do this – be sure to skip a number on your answer sheet as well. Check often to be sure that you have not lost your place and that you are marking in the row numbered the same as the question you are answering.

6) Read the questions

Be sure you know what the question asks! Many capable people are unsuccessful because they failed to *read* the questions correctly.

7) Answer all questions

Unless you have been instructed that a penalty will be deducted for incorrect answers, it is better to guess than to omit a question.

8) Speed tests

It is often better NOT to guess on speed tests. It has been found that on timed tests people are tempted to spend the last few seconds before time is called in marking answers at random – without even reading them – in the hope of picking up a few extra points. To discourage this practice, the instructions may warn you that your score will be "corrected" for guessing. That is, a penalty will be applied. The incorrect answers will be deducted from the correct ones, or some other penalty formula will be used.

9) Review your answers

If you finish before time is called, go back to the questions you guessed or omitted to give them further thought. Review other answers if you have time.

10) Return your test materials

If you are ready to leave before others have finished or time is called, take ALL your materials to the monitor and leave quietly. Never take any test material with you. The monitor can discover whose papers are not complete, and taking a test booklet may be grounds for disqualification.

VIII. EXAMINATION TECHNIQUES

1) Read the general instructions carefully. These are usually printed on the first page of the exam booklet. As a rule, these instructions refer to the timing of the examination; the fact that you should not start work until the signal and must stop work at a signal, etc. If there are any *special* instructions, such as a choice of questions to be answered, make sure that you note this instruction carefully.

2) When you are ready to start work on the examination, that is as soon as the signal has been given, read the instructions to each question booklet, underline any key words or phrases, such as *least, best, outline, describe* and the like. In this way you will tend to answer as requested rather than discover on reviewing your paper that you *listed without describing*, that you selected the *worst* choice rather than the *best* choice, etc.

3) If the examination is of the objective or multiple-choice type – that is, each question will also give a series of possible answers: A, B, C or D, and you are called upon to select the best answer and write the letter next to that answer on your answer paper – it is advisable to start answering each question in turn. There may be anywhere from 50 to 100 such questions in the three or four hours allotted and you can see how much time would be taken if you read through all the questions before beginning to answer any. Furthermore, if you come across a question or group of questions which you know would be difficult to answer, it would undoubtedly affect your handling of all the other questions.

4) If the examination is of the essay type and contains but a few questions, it is a moot point as to whether you should read all the questions before starting to answer any one. Of course, if you are given a choice – say five out of seven and the like – then it is essential to read all the questions so you can eliminate the two that are most difficult. If, however, you are asked to answer all the questions, there may be danger in trying to answer the easiest one first because you may find that you will spend too much time on it. The best technique is to answer the first question, then proceed to the second, etc.

5) Time your answers. Before the exam begins, write down the time it started, then add the time allowed for the examination and write down the time it must be completed, then divide the time available somewhat as follows:
    - If 3-1/2 hours are allowed, that would be 210 minutes. If you have 80 objective-type questions, that would be an average of 2-1/2 minutes per question. Allow yourself no more than 2 minutes per question, or a total of 160 minutes, which will permit about 50 minutes to review.
    - If for the time allotment of 210 minutes there are 7 essay questions to answer, that would average about 30 minutes a question. Give yourself only 25 minutes per question so that you have about 35 minutes to review.

6) The most important instruction is to *read each question* and make sure you know what is wanted. The second most important instruction is to *time yourself properly* so that you answer every question. The third most important instruction is to *answer every question*. Guess if you have to but include something for each question. Remember that you will receive no credit for a blank and will probably receive some credit if you write something in answer to an essay question. If you guess a letter – say "B" for a multiple-choice question – you may have guessed right. If you leave a blank as an answer to a multiple-choice question, the examiners may respect your feelings but it will not add a point to your score. Some exams may penalize you for wrong answers, so in such cases *only*, you may not want to guess unless you have some basis for your answer.

7) Suggestions
    a. Objective-type questions
        1. Examine the question booklet for proper sequence of pages and questions
        2. Read all instructions carefully
        3. Skip any question which seems too difficult; return to it after all other questions have been answered
        4. Apportion your time properly; do not spend too much time on any single question or group of questions

5. Note and underline key words – *all, most, fewest, least, best, worst, same, opposite,* etc.
6. Pay particular attention to negatives
7. Note unusual option, e.g., unduly long, short, complex, different or similar in content to the body of the question
8. Observe the use of "hedging" words – *probably, may, most likely,* etc.
9. Make sure that your answer is put next to the same number as the question
10. Do not second-guess unless you have good reason to believe the second answer is definitely more correct
11. Cross out original answer if you decide another answer is more accurate; do not erase until you are ready to hand your paper in
12. Answer all questions; guess unless instructed otherwise
13. Leave time for review

b. Essay questions
1. Read each question carefully
2. Determine exactly what is wanted. Underline key words or phrases.
3. Decide on outline or paragraph answer
4. Include many different points and elements unless asked to develop any one or two points or elements
5. Show impartiality by giving pros and cons unless directed to select one side only
6. Make and write down any assumptions you find necessary to answer the questions
7. Watch your English, grammar, punctuation and choice of words
8. Time your answers; don't crowd material

8) Answering the essay question

Most essay questions can be answered by framing the specific response around several key words or ideas. Here are a few such key words or ideas:

M's: manpower, materials, methods, money, management
P's: purpose, program, policy, plan, procedure, practice, problems, pitfalls, personnel, public relations

a. Six basic steps in handling problems:
1. Preliminary plan and background development
2. Collect information, data and facts
3. Analyze and interpret information, data and facts
4. Analyze and develop solutions as well as make recommendations
5. Prepare report and sell recommendations
6. Install recommendations and follow up effectiveness

b. Pitfalls to avoid
1. *Taking things for granted* – A statement of the situation does not necessarily imply that each of the elements is necessarily true; for example, a complaint may be invalid and biased so that all that can be taken for granted is that a complaint has been registered

2. *Considering only one side of a situation* – Wherever possible, indicate several alternatives and then point out the reasons you selected the best one
3. *Failing to indicate follow up* – Whenever your answer indicates action on your part, make certain that you will take proper follow-up action to see how successful your recommendations, procedures or actions turn out to be
4. *Taking too long in answering any single question* – Remember to time your answers properly

IX. AFTER THE TEST

Scoring procedures differ in detail among civil service jurisdictions although the general principles are the same. Whether the papers are hand-scored or graded by machine we have described, they are nearly always graded by number. That is, the person who marks the paper knows only the number – never the name – of the applicant. Not until all the papers have been graded will they be matched with names. If other tests, such as training and experience or oral interview ratings have been given, scores will be combined. Different parts of the examination usually have different weights. For example, the written test might count 60 percent of the final grade, and a rating of training and experience 40 percent. In many jurisdictions, veterans will have a certain number of points added to their grades.

After the final grade has been determined, the names are placed in grade order and an eligible list is established. There are various methods for resolving ties between those who get the same final grade – probably the most common is to place first the name of the person whose application was received first. Job offers are made from the eligible list in the order the names appear on it. You will be notified of your grade and your rank as soon as all these computations have been made. This will be done as rapidly as possible.

People who are found to meet the requirements in the announcement are called "eligibles." Their names are put on a list of eligible candidates. An eligible's chances of getting a job depend on how high he stands on this list and how fast agencies are filling jobs from the list.

When a job is to be filled from a list of eligibles, the agency asks for the names of people on the list of eligibles for that job. When the civil service commission receives this request, it sends to the agency the names of the three people highest on this list. Or, if the job to be filled has specialized requirements, the office sends the agency the names of the top three persons who meet these requirements from the general list.

The appointing officer makes a choice from among the three people whose names were sent to him. If the selected person accepts the appointment, the names of the others are put back on the list to be considered for future openings.

That is the rule in hiring from all kinds of eligible lists, whether they are for typist, carpenter, chemist, or something else. For every vacancy, the appointing officer has his choice of any one of the top three eligibles on the list. This explains why the person whose name is on top of the list sometimes does not get an appointment when some of the persons lower on the list do. If the appointing officer chooses the second or third eligible, the No. 1 eligible does not get a job at once, but stays on the list until he is appointed or the list is terminated.

X. HOW TO PASS THE INTERVIEW TEST

The examination for which you applied requires an oral interview test. You have already taken the written test and you are now being called for the interview test – the final part of the formal examination.

You may think that it is not possible to prepare for an interview test and that there are no procedures to follow during an interview. Our purpose is to point out some things you can do in advance that will help you and some good rules to follow and pitfalls to avoid while you are being interviewed.

What is an interview supposed to test?

The written examination is designed to test the technical knowledge and competence of the candidate; the oral is designed to evaluate intangible qualities, not readily measured otherwise, and to establish a list showing the relative fitness of each candidate – as measured against his competitors – for the position sought. Scoring is not on the basis of "right" and "wrong," but on a sliding scale of values ranging from "not passable" to "outstanding." As a matter of fact, it is possible to achieve a relatively low score without a single "incorrect" answer because of evident weakness in the qualities being measured.

Occasionally, an examination may consist entirely of an oral test – either an individual or a group oral. In such cases, information is sought concerning the technical knowledges and abilities of the candidate, since there has been no written examination for this purpose. More commonly, however, an oral test is used to supplement a written examination.

Who conducts interviews?

The composition of oral boards varies among different jurisdictions. In nearly all, a representative of the personnel department serves as chairman. One of the members of the board may be a representative of the department in which the candidate would work. In some cases, "outside experts" are used, and, frequently, a businessman or some other representative of the general public is asked to serve. Labor and management or other special groups may be represented. The aim is to secure the services of experts in the appropriate field.

However the board is composed, it is a good idea (and not at all improper or unethical) to ascertain in advance of the interview who the members are and what groups they represent. When you are introduced to them, you will have some idea of their backgrounds and interests, and at least you will not stutter and stammer over their names.

What should be done before the interview?

While knowledge about the board members is useful and takes some of the surprise element out of the interview, there is other preparation which is more substantive. It *is* possible to prepare for an oral interview – in several ways:

1) Keep a copy of your application and review it carefully before the interview

This may be the only document before the oral board, and the starting point of the interview. Know what education and experience you have listed there, and the sequence and dates of all of it. Sometimes the board will ask you to review the highlights of your experience for them; you should not have to hem and haw doing it.

2) Study the class specification and the examination announcement

Usually, the oral board has one or both of these to guide them. The qualities, characteristics or knowledges required by the position sought are stated in these documents. They offer valuable clues as to the nature of the oral interview. For example, if the job involves supervisory responsibilities, the announcement will usually indicate that knowledge of modern supervisory methods and the qualifications of the candidate as a supervisor will be tested. If so, you can expect such questions, frequently in the form of a hypothetical situation which you are expected to solve. NEVER go into an oral without knowledge of the duties and responsibilities of the job you seek.

3) Think through each qualification required

Try to visualize the kind of questions you would ask if you were a board member. How well could you answer them? Try especially to appraise your own knowledge and background in each area, *measured against the job sought*, and identify any areas in which you are weak. Be critical and realistic – do not flatter yourself.

4) Do some general reading in areas in which you feel you may be weak

For example, if the job involves supervision and your past experience has NOT, some general reading in supervisory methods and practices, particularly in the field of human relations, might be useful. Do NOT study agency procedures or detailed manuals. The oral board will be testing your understanding and capacity, not your memory.

5) Get a good night's sleep and watch your general health and mental attitude

You will want a clear head at the interview. Take care of a cold or any other minor ailment, and of course, no hangovers.

What should be done on the day of the interview?

Now comes the day of the interview itself. Give yourself plenty of time to get there. Plan to arrive somewhat ahead of the scheduled time, particularly if your appointment is in the fore part of the day. If a previous candidate fails to appear, the board might be ready for you a bit early. By early afternoon an oral board is almost invariably behind schedule if there are many candidates, and you may have to wait. Take along a book or magazine to read, or your application to review, but leave any extraneous material in the waiting room when you go in for your interview. In any event, relax and compose yourself.

The matter of dress is important. The board is forming impressions about you – from your experience, your manners, your attitude, and your appearance. Give your personal appearance careful attention. Dress your best, but not your flashiest. Choose conservative, appropriate clothing, and be sure it is immaculate. This is a business interview, and your appearance should indicate that you regard it as such. Besides, being well groomed and properly dressed will help boost your confidence.

Sooner or later, someone will call your name and escort you into the interview room. *This is it.* From here on you are on your own. It is too late for any more preparation. But remember, you asked for this opportunity to prove your fitness, and you are here because your request was granted.

What happens when you go in?

The usual sequence of events will be as follows: The clerk (who is often the board stenographer) will introduce you to the chairman of the oral board, who will introduce you to the other members of the board. Acknowledge the introductions before you sit down. Do not be surprised if you find a microphone facing you or a stenotypist sitting by. Oral interviews are usually recorded in the event of an appeal or other review.

Usually the chairman of the board will open the interview by reviewing the highlights of your education and work experience from your application – primarily for the benefit of the other members of the board, as well as to get the material into the record. Do not interrupt or comment unless there is an error or significant misinterpretation; if that is the case, do not hesitate. But do not quibble about insignificant matters. Also, he will usually ask you some question about your education, experience or your present job – partly to get you to start talking and to establish the interviewing "rapport." He may start the actual questioning, or turn it over to one of the other members. Frequently, each member undertakes the questioning on a particular area, one in which he is perhaps most competent, so you can expect each member to participate in the examination. Because time is limited, you may also expect some rather abrupt switches in the direction the questioning takes, so do not be upset by it. Normally, a board member will not pursue a single line of questioning unless he discovers a particular strength or weakness.

After each member has participated, the chairman will usually ask whether any member has any further questions, then will ask you if you have anything you wish to add. Unless you are expecting this question, it may floor you. Worse, it may start you off on an extended, extemporaneous speech. The board is not usually seeking more information. The question is principally to offer you a last opportunity to present further qualifications or to indicate that you have nothing to add. So, if you feel that a significant qualification or characteristic has been overlooked, it is proper to point it out in a sentence or so. Do not compliment the board on the thoroughness of their examination – they have been sketchy, and you know it. If you wish, merely say, "No thank you, I have nothing further to add." This is a point where you can "talk yourself out" of a good impression or fail to present an important bit of information. Remember, *you close the interview yourself.*

The chairman will then say, "That is all, Mr. _____, thank you." Do not be startled; the interview is over, and quicker than you think. Thank him, gather your belongings and take your leave. Save your sigh of relief for the other side of the door.

How to put your best foot forward

Throughout this entire process, you may feel that the board individually and collectively is trying to pierce your defenses, seek out your hidden weaknesses and embarrass and confuse you. Actually, this is not true. They are obliged to make an appraisal of your qualifications for the job you are seeking, and they want to see you in your best light. Remember, they must interview all candidates and a non-cooperative candidate may become a failure in spite of their best efforts to bring out his qualifications. Here are 15 suggestions that will help you:

1) Be natural – Keep your attitude confident, not cocky

If you are not confident that you can do the job, do not expect the board to be. Do not apologize for your weaknesses, try to bring out your strong points. The board is interested in a positive, not negative, presentation. Cockiness will antagonize any board member and make him wonder if you are covering up a weakness by a false show of strength.

2) Get comfortable, but don't lounge or sprawl

Sit erectly but not stiffly. A careless posture may lead the board to conclude that you are careless in other things, or at least that you are not impressed by the importance of the occasion. Either conclusion is natural, even if incorrect. Do not fuss with your clothing, a pencil or an ashtray. Your hands may occasionally be useful to emphasize a point; do not let them become a point of distraction.

3) Do not wisecrack or make small talk

This is a serious situation, and your attitude should show that you consider it as such. Further, the time of the board is limited – they do not want to waste it, and neither should you.

4) Do not exaggerate your experience or abilities

In the first place, from information in the application or other interviews and sources, the board may know more about you than you think. Secondly, you probably will not get away with it. An experienced board is rather adept at spotting such a situation, so do not take the chance.

5) If you know a board member, do not make a point of it, yet do not hide it

Certainly you are not fooling him, and probably not the other members of the board. Do not try to take advantage of your acquaintanceship – it will probably do you little good.

6) Do not dominate the interview

Let the board do that. They will give you the clues – do not assume that you have to do all the talking. Realize that the board has a number of questions to ask you, and do not try to take up all the interview time by showing off your extensive knowledge of the answer to the first one.

7) Be attentive

You only have 20 minutes or so, and you should keep your attention at its sharpest throughout. When a member is addressing a problem or question to you, give him your undivided attention. Address your reply principally to him, but do not exclude the other board members.

8) Do not interrupt

A board member may be stating a problem for you to analyze. He will ask you a question when the time comes. Let him state the problem, and wait for the question.

9) Make sure you understand the question

Do not try to answer until you are sure what the question is. If it is not clear, restate it in your own words or ask the board member to clarify it for you. However, do not haggle about minor elements.

10) Reply promptly but not hastily

A common entry on oral board rating sheets is "candidate responded readily," or "candidate hesitated in replies." Respond as promptly and quickly as you can, but do not jump to a hasty, ill-considered answer.

11) Do not be peremptory in your answers

A brief answer is proper – but do not fire your answer back. That is a losing game from your point of view. The board member can probably ask questions much faster than you can answer them.

12) Do not try to create the answer you think the board member wants

He is interested in what kind of mind you have and how it works – not in playing games. Furthermore, he can usually spot this practice and will actually grade you down on it.

13) Do not switch sides in your reply merely to agree with a board member

Frequently, a member will take a contrary position merely to draw you out and to see if you are willing and able to defend your point of view. Do not start a debate, yet do not surrender a good position. If a position is worth taking, it is worth defending.

14) Do not be afraid to admit an error in judgment if you are shown to be wrong

The board knows that you are forced to reply without any opportunity for careful consideration. Your answer may be demonstrably wrong. If so, admit it and get on with the interview.

15) Do not dwell at length on your present job

The opening question may relate to your present assignment. Answer the question but do not go into an extended discussion. You are being examined for a *new* job, not your present one. As a matter of fact, try to phrase ALL your answers in terms of the job for which you are being examined.

Basis of Rating

Probably you will forget most of these "do's" and "don'ts" when you walk into the oral interview room. Even remembering them all will not ensure you a passing grade. Perhaps you did not have the qualifications in the first place. But remembering them will help you to put your best foot forward, without treading on the toes of the board members.

Rumor and popular opinion to the contrary notwithstanding, an oral board wants you to make the best appearance possible. They know you are under pressure – but they also want to see how you respond to it as a guide to what your reaction would be under the pressures of the job you seek. They will be influenced by the degree of poise you display, the personal traits you show and the manner in which you respond.

ABOUT THIS BOOK

This book contains tests divided into Examination Sections. Go through each test, answering every question in the margin. We have also attached a sample answer sheet at the back of the book that can be removed and used. At the end of each test look at the answer key and check your answers. On the ones you got wrong, look at the right answer choice and learn. Do not fill in the answers first. Do not memorize the questions and answers, but understand the answer and principles involved. On your test, the questions will likely be different from the samples. Questions are changed and new ones added. If you understand these past questions you should have success with any changes that arise. Tests may consist of several types of questions. We have additional books on each subject should more study be advisable or necessary for you. Finally, the more you study, the better prepared you will be. This book is intended to be the last thing you study before you walk into the examination room. Prior study of relevant texts is also recommended. NLC publishes some of these in our Fundamental Series. Knowledge and good sense are important factors in passing your exam. Good luck also helps. So now study this Passbook, absorb the material contained within and take that knowledge into the examination. Then do your best to pass that exam.

EXAMINATION SECTION

EXAMINATION SECTION
TEST 1

DIRECTIONS: Each question or incomplete statement is followed by several suggested answers or completions. Select the one that BEST answers the question or completes the statement. *PRINT THE LETTER OF THE CORRECT ANSWER IN THE SPACE AT THE RIGHT.*

1. Elevator car safeties are set to function

    A. in the direction determined by the installer
    B. in either the up or the down direction
    C. *only* in the down direction
    D. *only* in the up direction

    1.____

2. Of the following, the BEST type of fire extinguisher to use on an electrical fire is

    A. water type stored pressure
    B. carbon dioxide
    C. soda-acid
    D. foam

    2.____

3. The purpose of a rectifier is to

    A. step down 440 voltage to 220 voltage
    B. function as a starting resistance for D.C. hoist motors
    C. change alternating current to direct current
    D. stop up voltage

    3.____

4. The property of a material that tends to prevent the flow of electric current through it is known as

    A. flux
    C. elasticity
    B. resistance
    D. excitation

    4.____

5. The automatic terminal stopping devices are USUALLY located in the

    A. flexible guide clamp assembly
    B. hoistway
    C. motor brake
    D. inside of the cab

    5.____

6. When using an uninsulated portable electric tool in a damp location, the hazard of an electric shock can BEST be lessened by making sure that the

    A. person using the tool is grounded
    B. tool is dry
    C. tool is grounded
    D. tool is used only with a 110-volt electric supply

    6.____

7. The terminal limit switches are USUALLY operated by the

    A. cams
    C. hydraulic pressure
    B. tiller rope
    D. air pressure

    7.____

8. A tool COMMONLY used to cut holes in masonry is the

   A. plane
   B. auger bit
   C. bottoming taps
   D. star drill

9. An ammeter measures

   A. watts
   B. resistance
   C. current
   D. voltage

10. A die is a tool used to cut

    A. external threads
    B. internal threads
    C. conduit
    D. broken screws

11. The BEST type of fasteners to use when mounting outlet boxes onto a concrete wall are

    A. sheet metal screws
    B. toggle bolts
    C. U-bolts
    D. expansion screw anchors

12. A VOM would be used to measure

    A. motor speed
    B. electricity
    C. brake pressure
    D. air pressure

13. The state of the charge in a lead-acid storage battery would be checked by a

    A. psychrometer
    B. interferometer
    C. calorimeter
    D. hydrometer

14. The one of the following which should be used to pull several wires at one time into a conduit is the _____ grip.

    A. basket   B. tie   C. box   D. knuckle

15. When an ammeter is used to test an electric circuit, the instrument should be connected

    A. across the line
    B. in parallel with the circuit
    C. in series with the circuit
    D. either in parallel or series with the circuit

16. The one of the following dimensions of a wire that would be measured with a micrometer is the

    A. diameter
    B. area
    C. circumference
    D. length

17. The one of the following instruments used when making a speed-load test is the

    A. tachometer
    B. potentiometer
    C. speedometer
    D. petrometer

18. When cutting non-preformed wire rope, the number of seizings that should be made on each side of the cut is

    A. three   B. four   C. five   D. six

19. *BX* is the term sometimes used in referring to   19.____

    A. armored cable   B. lead sleeves
    C. sheet metal strips   D. wire rope

20. The tool used to drive a lag screw is a(n)   20.____

    A. screwdriver   B. Stillson wrench
    C. Allen wrench   D. open end wrench

21. A metal washer is MOST generally used with a   21.____

    A. flat head wood screw   B. carriage bolt
    C. set screw   D. machine screw

22. A circuit breaker serves the same purpose as a   22.____

    A. relay   B. solenoid   C. fuse   D. switch

23. Heat generated by dynamic braking is dissipated through   23.____

    A. rectifiers   B. dashpots
    C. relays   D. resistors

24. The one of the following items which can BEST be inspected from the top of the elevator car is a   24.____

    A. door operating device   B. M.G. starter
    C. governor flyball weight D. brake shoe

25. Of the following, the one which is MOST frequently used to loosen a rusted bolt is   25.____

    A. graphite   B. a mixture of graphite and oil
    C. linseed oil   D. penetrating oil

26. A spring is sometimes used in connection with an electrical contact MAINLY to   26.____

    A. dissipate the heat arising from the contact
    B. reduce the resistance at the contact
    C. bring current to the contact
    D. act as a shunt to carry high currents

27. A broken chain test is MOST frequently performed on a(n)   27.____

    A. gearless traction machine   B. overhead drum machine
    C. escalator   D. basement drum machine

28. The MAIN purpose of a reverse-phase relay is to protect the   28.____

    A. hoist motor against reversal   B. signal system
    C. faces of the contacts   D. governor contract load

29. In general, an elevator brake should be adjusted so that its shoes _____ the brake drum.

    A. have a clearance of 0.40" from
    B. have a clearance of 0.28" from
    C. have a clearance of 0.20" from
    D. just clear

30. A 6x19 wire rope is one which

    A. has 19 strands of 6 wires each
    B. has 6 strands of 19 wires each
    C. is always a regular-lay rope
    D. is always a lang-lay rope

31. The transmission of car motion to the governor rope is performed by the

    A. rheostatic control
    B. normal terminal stop device
    C. releasing carrier
    D. generator-field control

32. When examining an elevator cable for broken wires, it is MOST important that a mechanic use a

    A. piece of chalk
    B. flashlight
    C. voltmeter
    D. shunt

33. It is BEST to lubricate elevator machinery

    A. on a regular schedule
    B. only when lubrication is needed
    C. whenever it is determined that the oil is running low
    D. when severe vibration occurs

34. An elevator mechanic generally checks for excessive *backlash* in a

    A. buffer   B. hoist   C. bearing   D. gear

35. The governor tension weight or sheave is generally located

    A. in the penthouse
    B. near the governor
    C. in the pit
    D. on the side of the car

KEY (CORRECT ANSWERS)

1. C	11. D	21. D
2. B	12. B	22. C
3. C	13. D	23. D
4. B	14. A	24. A
5. B	15. C	25. D
6. C	16. A	26. B
7. A	17. A	27. C
8. D	18. A	28. A
9. C	19. A	29. D
10. A	20. D	30. B

31. C
32. B
33. A
34. D
35. C

TEST 2

DIRECTIONS: Each question or incomplete statement is followed by several suggested answers or completions. Select the one that BEST answers the question or completes the statement. *PRINT THE LETTER OF THE CORRECT ANSWER IN THE SPACE AT THE RIGHT.*

1. In elevator operation, the term *landing zone* means the space within a distance above or below the landing of _____ inches.

    A. 4 B. 8 C. 18 D. 40

2. Cable equalizers are installed on traction elevators in order to

    A. equalize the load on each cable
    B. prevent over-travel of the car
    C. keep all cables the same length
    D. reduce the need for manual inspection of cables

3. The one of the following that is PROPER to use to dress a motor commutator is

    A. a flat file
    B. emery cloth
    C. a mill file
    D. sandpaper

4. The inductor plates in an elevator installation are generally located

    A. near the worm and gear housing
    B. near the buffers
    C. in the hoistway
    D. in the machine room

5. The PROPER position of the brushes on a D.C. motor commutator is on, or close to, _____ position.

    A. the one-half
    B. the neutral
    C. the one-quarter
    D. 20° off the neutral

6. The MAXIMUM permitted contact arc between the ropes and sheave in a single-wrap traction machine is

    A. 180° B. 200° C. 230° D. 260°

7. The one of the following that may be considered to be a miniature elevator is the

    A. safety plank
    B. overhead crosshead
    C. cab enclosure
    D. floor selector

8. Compared to a D.C. elevator brake of the same capacity and speed, an A.C. elevator brake is _____ the D.C. brake.

    A. the same size as
    B. smoother in operation than
    C. considerably larger than
    D. smaller than

9. In elevator installations, the potential switch is USUALLY found in the _____ circuit.　9.____

   A. condenser   B. lighting   C. safety   D. rectifier

10. The USUAL location of thrust bearings is on the　10.____

    A. reverse phase relays   B. governor safety jaws
    C. worm shaft   D. buffer

11. The purpose of the flux in a soldering operation is to　11.____

    A. keep the surfaces of the work clean
    B. spread the heat evenly to all parts of the work
    C. lubricate the gun tip
    D. roughen the surfaces of the work

12. Comb-plates are GENERALLY found on　12.____

    A. car overheads   B. selectors
    C. traveling cables   D. escalators

13. Ohm's Law relating current, voltage, and resistance is　13.____

    A. $E = IR$ B. $F = WD$ C. $F = MA$ D. $E = \frac{1}{R}$

14. The power lost in a field rheostat in a D.C. circuit is 125 watts with a resistance of 5 ohms.
    The current, in amperes, in the rheostat is　14.____

    A. 2.0   B. 2.5   C. 3.5   D. 5.0

15. The one of the following that is the BEST conductor of electricity is　15.____

    A. iron   B. aluminum   C. manganin   D. tin

16. The equivalent resistance, in ohms, of a circuit having three resistances, respectively 4, 5, and 10 ohms, in parallel is MOST NEARLY　16.____

    A. 4.5   B. 2.4   C. 1.8   D. 1.1

17. On elevators, the emergency release switch is used　17.____

    A. to make the door electric contacts or door interlocks inoperative
    B. to override the emergency stop switch
    C. by passengers in an emergency if the emergency stop switch is inoperative
    D. to cut off the power

18. The one of the following devices which automatically levels the elevator car at the landings is the　18.____

    A. limit switch   B. brake assembly
    C. governor   D. floor selector

19. Of the following electrical services, the one that is MOST likely to be polyphase is　19.____

    A. 2-wire, 120-volt A.C.   B. 2-wire, 115-volt B.C.
    C. 3-wire, 110/208-volt D.C.   D. 4-wire, 120/208-volt A.C.

20. When 0.750 is divided by 0.875, the result is MOST NEARLY 20.____

   A. 0.250 B. 0.312 C. 0.624 D. 0.857

21. The circumference of a 6-inch diameter circle is MOST NEARLY _____ feet. 21.____

   A. 1.57 B. 2.1 C. 2.31 D. 4.24

22. An 18" piece of cable that weighs 3 lbs. per foot has a total weight of _____ lbs. 22.____

   A. 5.5 B. 4.5 C. 3.0 D. 1.5

23. The sum of 0.135, 0.040, 0.812, and 0.961 is 23.____

   A. 1.424 B. 1.625 C. 1.843 D. 1.948

24. If an elevator carries a load of 1600 pounds uniformly distributed on a 4 feet by 5 feet floor, the weight per square foot is _____ pounds. 24.____

   A. 98 B. 80 C. 65 D. 40

25. If one cubic inch of lead weighs one-quarter of a pound, the weight of a bar of lead 1" high by 2" wide by 8" long is _____ lbs. 25.____

   A. 1.8 B. 2.5 C. 3.1 D. 4

26. A *2-to-1* roping of an elevator installation means that the rope speed is _____ the car speed. 26.____

   A. twice
   B. one-half
   C. one-quarter of
   D. one-eighth of

27. The one of the following which is NOT an indication of trouble in an electric motor or generator is that the 27.____

   A. vent holes are clogged
   B. commutator has flat spots
   C. armature is oil-soaked
   D. mica is undercut

28. Oil levels in buffers should be checked by an employee 28.____

   A. when he is available to check them
   B. at regular intervals
   C. daily
   D. only when the elevator is operating

29. Assume that the lift of an elevator is 275 feet from the bottom landing to the top landing. If the car takes 30 seconds to travel this distance in one direction, the car speed, in feet per minute, is 29.____

   A. 550 B. 450 C. 350 D. 275

30. In a rheostatic controller, speed control is achieved MAINLY through the use of 30.____

　　A. capacitors　　　　　　　　　B. resistors
　　C. condensers　　　　　　　　　D. diodes

Questions 31-35.

DIRECTIONS: Questions 31 through 35, inclusive, are to be answered in accordance with the paragraph below.

Panelboards are used to serve branch circuits to lamps, motors, elevators, or other electrical equipment. It is an <u>insulated</u> panel on which are mounted, with some degree of symmetry, various switches and circuit breakers. One <u>terminal</u> of each switch is wired to the bus bars of the panelboard, the other terminal of the switch is connected to the protective device. The bus bars of the panelboard are <u>energized</u> by a feeder which brings service to the panel from another part of the building. Panelboards are classified as flush type, service type, or by the number of wires in the feeder and branch circuit systems. Deadfront panelboards that have insulated <u>manually</u> operated main and branch breaker handles should always be used for safety reasons.

31. The word <u>insulated</u>, as used in the above paragraph, means MOST NEARLY 31.____

　　A. non-conducting　　　　　　B. instrument
　　C. open　　　　　　　　　　　D. wall

32. The word <u>terminal</u>, as used in the above paragraph, means MOST NEARLY 32.____

　　A. wire　　　B. connector　　　C. side　　　D. overload

33. The word <u>energized</u>, as used in the above paragraph, means MOST NEARLY 33.____

　　A. enfolded　　　　　　　　　B. enervated
　　C. receded　　　　　　　　　　D. electrified

34. The word <u>manually</u>, as used in the above paragraph, means MOST NEARLY 34.____

　　A. block　　　B. hand　　　C. relay　　　D. power

35. The number of types of classifications of panelboards is 35.____

　　A. 1　　　B. 2　　　C. 3　　　D. 4

KEY (CORRECT ANSWERS)

1.	C	11.	A	21.	A
2.	A	12.	D	22.	B
3.	D	13.	A	23.	D
4.	C	14.	D	24.	B
5.	B	15.	B	25.	D
6.	A	16.	C	26.	A
7.	D	17.	A	27.	D
8.	C	18.	D	28.	B
9.	C	19.	D	29.	A
10.	C	20.	D	30.	B
		31.	A		
		32.	B		
		33.	D		
		34.	C		
		35.	B		

EXAMINATION SECTION
TEST 1

DIRECTIONS: Each question or incomplete statement is followed by several suggested answers or completions. Select the one that BEST answers the question or completes the statement. *PRINT THE LETTER OF THE CORRECT ANSWER IN THE SPACE AT THE RIGHT.*

1. Elevator machinery and related equipment is BEST lubricated   1.____

   A. whenever it is required
   B. after a shut-down
   C. during slack work periods
   D. at scheduled times

2. The direction of rotation of a D.C. shunt motor can be *reversed* by reversing   2.____

   A. the line connections
   B. both the field and the armature connections
   C. either the field or the armature connections
   D. the residual field

3. The bearings of geared type hoist motors are MOST usually of the _____ type.   3.____

   A. sleeve   B. ball bearing
   C. ball and roller   D. tapered roller

4. Installation of a Type A (instantaneous) car safety is limited to cars operating at speeds, in FPM, between _____ and _____.   4.____

   A. 0; 120   B. 130; 150   C. 175; 300   D. 150; 500

5. Of the following statements concerning the use of rubber-tired roller guides, the one which is MOST NEARLY correct is that their use would   5.____

   A. increase electric power usage
   B. help prevent hoistway fires
   C. increase maintenance costs
   D. require lubrication of the rails

6. Of the following grades of carbon steel wire rope, the one which contains the LEAST percentage of carbon is   6.____

   A. traction   B. improved plow
   C. plow   D. iron

7. In checking the neutral position of the carbon brushes in a variable voltage elevator hoist motor, a voltohmmeter is to be used as a test meter.
   Of the following meter scales, the CORRECT one to use would be the _____ scale.   7.____

   A. 50-microamp   B. 10-milliamp
   C. 10-amp   D. 15-amp

8. The rating of a standard cartridge fuse having a navy blue paper label is   8.____

2 (#1)

    A. 250 volts, 30 amperes capacity
    B. 250 volts, 15 amperes or less capacity
    C. 250 volts, over 15 amperes capacity
    D. 120 volts, 15 amperes capacity

9. In ordering a standard cartridge fuse, it is MOST necessary to specify the

    A. minimum length of ferrule and outside diameter of tube
    B. power factor of the connected load
    C. voltage of the circuit and the current capacity
    D. type of construction and the tolerance

10. Of the following substances, the BEST one to use to make it easier to pull wire conductors through electric conduit is

    A. powdered soapstone   B. petroleum jelly
    C. light oil   D. powdered graphite

11. A *Brinell test* is used to determine the

    A. hardness of metals
    B. strength of carbon brushes
    C. accuracy of tachometers
    D. number of broken wires in a rope

12. Of the following materials, the one which is NOT commonly used to line elevator brake shoes is

    A. asbestos   B. leather   C. wood   D. teflon

13. In a worm and gear elevator machine, metallic contact between the worm and the gear teeth is LEAST likely to occur when the oil level in the gear case is

    A. touching the bottom of the worm
    B. level with the center line of the worm-shaft
    C. level with the gear case drain plug
    D. between the bottom of the gear case and the bottom of the worm

14. The diameter of the hole of a bronze sleeve bearing is
$2.402"\, {}^{+.006"}_{-.000"}$ and the diameter of the shaft for this bearing is $2.401"\, {}^{+.000"}_{-.003"}$.
The limits of the clearance for the shaft in the bearing are MOST NEARLY _____" max; _____" min.

    A. .010; .001   B. .001; .001
    C. .007; .004   D. .006; .003

15. Of the following, the PRIMARY purpose of assigning mechanics to perform periodic inspection and testing of elevator equipment is to

    A. keep the mechanics active during slack periods
    B. provide on-the-job training for the less experienced mechanics

C. evaluate the mechanics' knowledge of the equipment
D. uncover potential equipment faults before they develop into major breakdowns

16. Of the following lubricants, the BEST one to use to lubricate elevator traction machine wire ropes is a

    A. heavy body oil mixed with graphite
    B. heavy body oil mixed with sulphur
    C. thin to medium heavy petroleum oil mixed with animal or vegetable oil
    D. very thin opaque oil mixed with a small quantity of pine tar

17. A megger tester is an instrument that is used to

    A. measure electrical insulation resistance
    B. determine the resistance of a bare copper conductor
    C. measure the rotative speed of a shaft
    D. determine the value of capacitors

18. When a mechanic is trained for a particular job, it is important that the mechanic be instructed properly. Listed below are four basic steps, in scrambled order, in training a worker:
    I. Demonstrate the actual operation to the mechanic
    II. Periodically check on the mechanic's performance
    III. Have the mechanic practice the job himself
    IV. Interest the mechanic in the job

    The CORRECT order in which these steps should be taken is

    A. II, I, III, IV
    B. III, I, IV, II
    C. II, IV, I, III
    D. IV, I, III, II

19. A suggestion is made that a machine be installed in the shop to help the mechanics on the job. You feel that the suggestion is a good one but realize that you cannot get the machine immediately, but that you may be able to obtain one at a later date.
    Of the following, the MOST effective way to handle the situation is to tell the mechanic that

    A. it is a good idea and to remind you of the suggestion at some other time
    B. you will look into the possibility and let him know if and when one can be installed
    C. the suggestion cannot be considered at the present time
    D. the shop does not require the machine and that none will be installed

20. One of the mechanics has just touched a bare electric wire carrying power and cannot let go.
    The one of the following actions that should be taken FIRST to assist the injured man is to

    A. use a dry rope or dry stick to remove the victim from the electrical source
    B. treat the mechanic for burns
    C. start artificial respiration or mouth-to-mouth breathing
    D. cut off the power, but only if it takes 5 minutes or less to find the switch

21. When lifting heavy objects without mechanical equipment, it is SAFEST to

    A. keep your back bent and knees straight

B. keep your feet as far from the object as possible
C. lift the object as fast as possible
D. use both arm and leg muscle

22. Of the following, the CHIEF cause of accidents on the job is

    A. faulty construction of elevator shafts
    B. mechanical failure of work equipment
    C. unsafe acts on the part of the workers
    D. improper work schedules

23. Assume that the men are being trained in the safe use of the ladder.
    According to accepted safety practice, if you place a 12-foot ladder against a wall, the distance between the foot of the ladder and the wall should be MOST NEARLY _____ foot(feet).

    A. 1   B. 3   C. 6   D. 9

24. Of the following types of portable fire extinguishers, the one which is the MOST suitable type for putting out *live* electrical wiring fires is a Class _____ extinguisher.

    A. A   B. B   C. C   D. D

25. Assume that you have been asked by the superintendent of a housing project to participate in a tenants' meeting regarding elevator vandalism.
    Of the following types of meetings, the one that will MOST likely have the highest tenant participation is the _____ type meeting.

    A. speaker-and-panel   B. formal conference
    C. open-discussion   D. speaker-only

KEY (CORRECT ANSWERS)

1. D		11. A	
2. C		12. D	
3. A		13. B	
4. A		14. A	
5. B		15. D	
6. D		16. C	
7. B		17. A	
8. B		18. D	
9. C		19. B	
10. A		20. A	

21. D
22. C
23. B
24. C
25. C

TEST 2

DIRECTIONS: Each question or incomplete statement is followed by several suggested answers or completions. Select the one that BEST answers the question or completes the statement. *PRINT THE LETTER OF THE CORRECT ANSWER IN THE SPACE AT THE RIGHT.*

1. The traveling crosshead or nut of a selector machine is driven vertically up and down by a

    A. flexible connection between the driving sheave and the car
    B. magnetically operated switch located on each landing
    C. steel tape attached to the car and wound on the sheaves at the top of the hoistway
    D. series of cold-cathode tubes electrically connected to a metal strip installed on the leading edge of the car door

    1._____

2. Assume that 8 mechanics have been assigned to do a job that must be finished in 5 days. At the end of 3 days, the men have completed only half the job.
   In order to complete the job on time in the remaining 2 days, the MINIMUM number of extra men that should be assigned is

    A. 2   B. 3   C. 4   D. 6

    2._____

3. Assume that the air gap between the stator and the bottom of the rotor of an A.C. motor is 0.01" less than a previously recorded clearance.
   This lessening of the air gap would MOST likely indicate that the

    A. spring tension holding the carbon brushes is excessive
    B. bearings of the motor are wearing
    C. stator laminations need to be replaced
    D. terminal voltage to the motor is too high

    3._____

4. Of the following types of wire-rope construction, the one recommended for double-wrap traction machines with sheaves under 30 inches in diameter is the

    A. 6 x 19 Warrington   B. 6 x 27 Regular
    C. 8 x 19 Seale   D. 8 x 25 Filler

    4._____

5. Upon inspecting an electrical contact in an elevator control circuit, you notice that the contact has a coating that is a dark bluish-black color.
   For this particular contact, it would be BEST to

    A. dress the contact by filing lightly with a double-cut smooth file
    B. mechanically open and close the contact periodically to break up the coating
    C. wipe the contact with a soft cloth
    D. leave the coating on the contact since it is a good conductor

    5._____

6. In a worm-gear elevator machine, the gear is GENERALLY machined from castings made of

    A. bronze   B. alloy steel   C. cast iron   D. copper

    6._____

7. An elevator supply manufacturer quotes a list price of $625 less 10 and 5 percent for ten contactors.
   The actual cost for these ten contactors is MOST NEARLY

    7._____

A. $562   B. $554   C. $534   D. $522

8. Assume that a rectifier has been disconnected from a circuit. Of the following meters, the one which should be used in checking the serviceability of this rectifier is a(n)

   A. ohmmeter
   C. ammeter
   B. AC voltmeter
   D. DC voltmeter

8._____

9. The length of a wire rope lay is APPROXIMATELY equal to _____ times the diameter of the rope.

   A. $3\frac{1}{2}$ B. $4\frac{1}{2}$ C. $5\frac{1}{2}$ D. $6\frac{1}{2}$

9._____

10. A generator that develops the same voltage at no load and at maximum load, but with a peak voltage in between, is called a(n) _____ compounded generator.

    A. differential   B. under   C. over   D. flat

10._____

Questions 11-17.

DIRECTIONS: Questions 11 to 17 are to be answered in accordance with the diagram shown below.

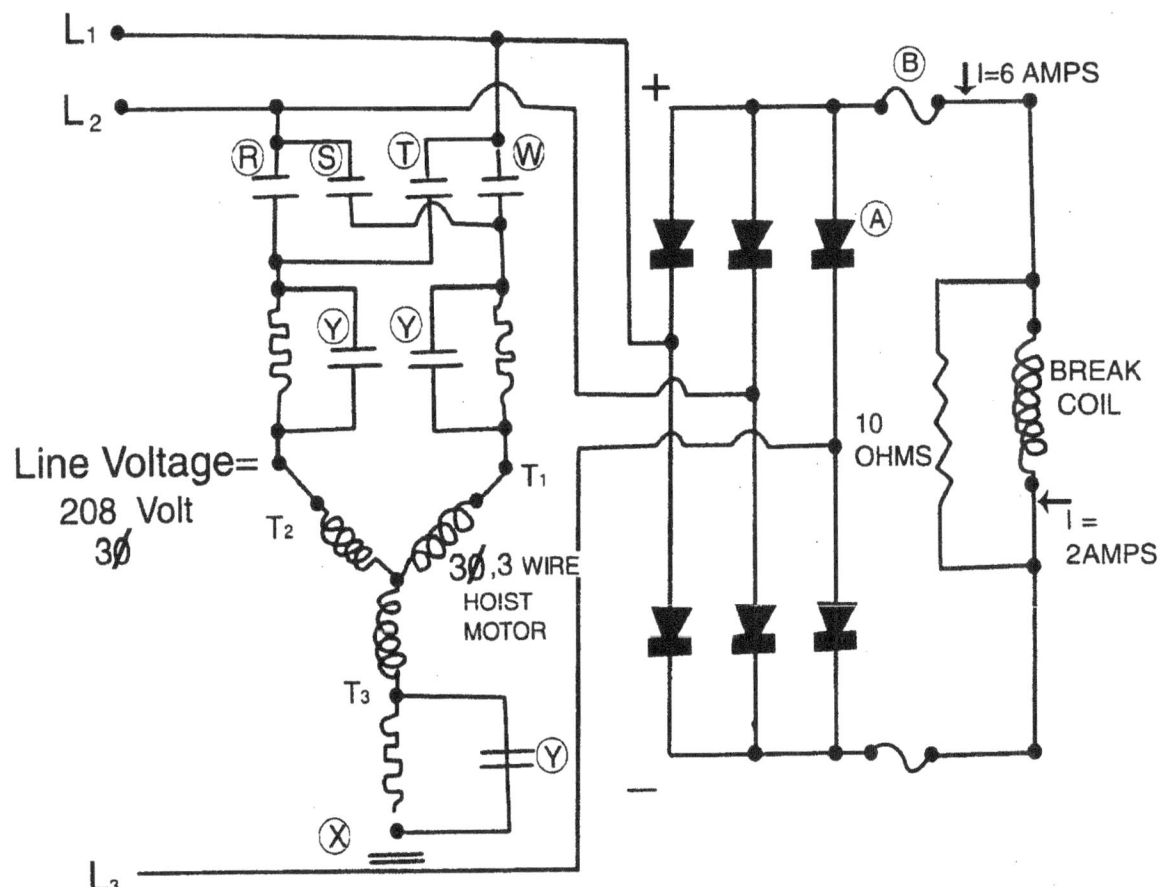

11. Each of the three contacts labeled Y in the above diagram are across a resistor. With respect to the operation of the hoist motor, these contacts should be

    A. closed when starting, open when running
    B. open when starting, closed when running
    C. closed when stopping, open when running
    D. open when stopping, open when running

12. Symbols such as the one labeled A in the above diagram USUALLY represent

    A. limit switches
    B. detectors
    C. interlocks
    D. rectifiers

13. The voltage across each of the hoist motor's three stator windings in the above diagram, when connected directly across the line, is MOST NEARLY _____ volts.

    A. 104   B. 120   C. 208   D. 416

14. Assume that the 3-phase hoist motor runs clockwise when contactors R, W, and X are closed, and contacts S and T are open.
    Of the following conditions, the one which will cause the motor to rotate in the OPPOSITE direction is

    A. open R, W, and X, close S and T
    B. open R, S, and T, close W and X
    C. close S, T, and X, open R and W
    D. close R, T, and W, open S and X

15. In the above diagram, the combined resistance of the brake coil and the 10-ohm resistor is MOST NEARLY _____ ohms.

    A. 5   B. 6 2/3   C. 10   D. 16 2/3

16. In the above diagram, the resistance of the brake coil is MOST NEARLY _____ ohms.

    A. zero   B. 10   C. 20   D. 30

17. In the above diagram, if the current through the fuse B is 6 amps, as shown, and the current through the brake coil is 2 amps, the voltage across the brake coil will be MOST NEARLY _____ volts.

    A. 2
    B. 4
    C. 10
    D. none of the above

18. Assume that you are meeting with a tenant group to explain a new, improved system of elevator maintenance for their building.
    Of the following, the LEAST effective method of maintaining the interest of this group is to

    A. concentrate only on the disadvantages of old elevator maintenance services
    B. show them how the new maintenance service will benefit them
    C. let them know what areas of the new maintenance plan you will discuss
    D. use visual aids to explain the new elevator maintenance service

19. Assume that, at a meeting with a tenant group, you are leading an open discussion on finding ways to reduce vandalism to the project's elevators.
Of the following practices, the BEST one for you to follow in leading the discussion is to

    A. make your suggestions, then give the group a chance to make theirs
    B. comment on and evaluate the contributions of members of the group to the discussion
    C. tell the group how they should operate as a discussion group
    D. encourage members of the group to speak out on the matter

20. You are asked to speak on ways to combat vandalism at a community housing project meeting.
Of the following, the BEST way to assure that the audience remembers the main points of your speech is to

    A. ask someone in the audience to read a written summary of the speech before you start speaking
    B. summarize the major points of your discussion at the end of your speech
    C. take a break during your speech and summarize the entire speech so far
    D. repeat what you have said every few paragraphs

21. The one of the following that is the MOST important characteristic of communication is that it

    A. involves just the sending of messages from one person to another
    B. transmits both information and understanding from one person to another
    C. helps the men adjust to work rules and procedures
    D. is concerned with the writing of clear, easy-to-read statements

22. The following are four important steps, in scrambled order, in the planning of a work project:
    I. Schedule the work
    II. Gather the facts
    III. Define the problem
    IV. Evaluate the facts

    The CORRECT order in which these steps should be taken to do the work project properly is

    A. III, II, IV, I   B. IV, III, II, I
    C. I, III, II, IV   D. II, III, IV, I

23. The one of the following that is commonly considered to be the MOST serious result of a mechanic's being frequently absent is that

    A. the supervisor may become unconcerned about the employee
    B. the employee in question may worry about his being late
    C. work schedules may be disrupted
    D. re-training of the employee will be necessary

24. Of the following, the BEST way to reduce the number of rumors related to work matters among mechanics is for supervisors to

    A. have the mechanics publish a bulletin describing all rumors presently circulating so that everything is *out in the open*
    B. supply accurate information to the mechanics as soon as possible on matters that are important to them
    C. constantly change their official interpretations of work matters so that the mechanics will not have any basis for rumors
    D. informally confide in their mechanics more often

25. According to the standard procedure manual, the symbol *N*, when used to record overtime work in the elevator log book, indicates

    A. night work differential
    B. nuisance
    C. necessary approval was granted
    D. no materials used

KEY (CORRECT ANSWERS)

1.	C	11.	B
2.	C	12.	D
3.	B	13.	B
4.	C	14.	C
5.	D	15.	B
6.	A	16.	C
7.	C	17.	D
8.	A	18.	A
9.	D	19.	D
10.	D	20.	B

21.	B
22.	A
23.	C
24.	B
25.	B

EXAMINATION SECTION
TEST 1

DIRECTIONS: Each question or incomplete statement is followed by several suggested answers or completions. Select the one that BEST answers the question or completes the statement. *PRINT THE LETTER OF THE CORRECT ANSWER IN THE SPACE AT THE RIGHT.*

1. Two or more elevator cars can be coordinated so that each answers its own car calls and all hall calls coming from a given portion of the building.
   This type of operation is known as   1.____

   A. zoning
   B. group dispatching
   C. on-call service
   D. zone-space operation

2. The MOST important reason for posting a Certificate of Inspection in an elevator is to   2.____

   A. instruct passengers to stand clear of the door
   B. inform passengers of the number of persons permitted to ride in the car
   C. prevent crowding at the car door
   D. assure the elevator mechanic that the elevator is in proper operating condition

3. Elevator *buffers* are designed to   3.____

   A. bring the car and counterweights to a smooth stop
   B. prevent the elevator doors from jamming
   C. prevent the elevator cars from shaking sideways
   D. separate one elevator from another

4. *Zoning* is used during periods of   4.____

   A. extremely light up or down peak traffic
   B. extremely heavy up or down peak traffic
   C. up peak service operation only
   D. down peak service operation only

5. If a fully loaded car always skips floor calls during peak periods of traffic, the MOST likely cause is   5.____

   A. automatic by-pass of the floors
   B. a weak or faulty cable
   C. a misfunction in the call-button system
   D. improper wiring of the control panel

6. Elevator *buffers* are located   6.____

   A. in the motor room
   B. on the top of the elevator car
   C. in the elevator pit
   D. on the car guard rails

7. That portion of a floor, balcony, or platform used to receive and discharge passengers or freight is usually known as the elevator _____ zone.   7.____

   A. landing   B. leveling   C. service   D. operating

8. A device which, when operated, will prevent the elevator from making a registered landing stop is called a

    A. non-stop switch
    B. governor
    C. limit switch
    D. gravity switch

9. All of the following are safety devices EXCEPT

    A. a governor
    B. a limit switch
    C. the interlocks
    D. a selector switch

10. The load-weighing device for automatic cars is located

    A. in the car pit
    B. beneath the elevator car platform
    C. in the control panel
    D. in the elevator mechanic's room

11. The MAIN purpose of the load-weighing device of an automatic elevator is to

    A. prevent operation of a crowded car
    B. speed up service
    C. keep the weight of the elevator constant
    D. open the door when an elevator is becoming overloaded

12. A device which is designed to prevent the movement of an automatic elevator car until the hoistway doors are mechanically locked in the closed position is known as the

    A. electronic switch
    B. interlock
    C. brake drum
    D. door-detector

13. The MAIN purpose of the photo-electric tube system in an elevator is to

    A. protect passengers
    B. assure a level landing
    C. prevent excessive speed
    D. control passenger load

14. The lights on the panelboard which show at which landings and for which direction elevator hall stop-or-signal calls are registered but unanswered are usually known as the _____ indicators.

    A. waiting passenger
    B. car position
    C. hall position
    D. landing

15. A cable made up of electric conductors, which provides electrical connections between an elevator car and a fixed outlet in the hoistway is known as the _____ cable.

    A. BX
    B. signal-transfer
    C. traveling
    D. registering

16. The devices mounted on the leading edges of the car doors to stop and reopen the doors if they touch a person or object are called

    A. safety shoes
    B. photo-electric rays
    C. door buffers
    D. emergency stop switches

17. If an elevator begins to overspeed, the device which is designed to open a safety switch and cut off power to the hoisting machine is the

    A. governor
    B. fuse
    C. controller
    D. speed limit interlock

18. *Peak-service operation* is a term usually used to describe an operation in which

    A. cars are dispatched to favor service in the direction of heavy travel
    B. cars take all passengers from their floors to the lobby without intermediate stops
    C. cars in reserve are automatically returned to the bottom terminal
    D. the starter controls the movements and direction of the cars' travel

19. *Time-space operation* is a term usually used to describe an operation in which cars are dispatched

    A. in one direction to favor service in that direction
    B. continuously in both directions to serve all passengers in minimum time
    C. in the direction of heavy travel only
    D. from the upper terminal at proper intervals to suit traffic

20. *Automatic car operation* is a term usually used to describe an operation in which each elevator is *automatically*

    A. controlled to stop in response to the car or hall calls for service in its direction of travel
    B. controlled to bypass certain floors in order to prevent delay at the bottom terminal
    C. controlled to bypass all hall calls
    D. dispatched to the upper floors with a full load

21. The operation that prevents service delay by a passenger who blocks the elevator door is known as

    A. bucking
    B. door detecting
    C. nudging
    D. dodging

22. In a photo-electric tube system, restoration of the light rays indicates that the car entrance is clear and the

    A. doors will stay open until the light ray is interrupted by a passenger
    B. doors are allowed to close
    C. elevator is empty
    D. elevator is moving upward

23. The term *premature* in connection with elevator doors refers to doors

    A. opening before the car is level with the landing
    B. closing before passengers enter the car
    C. opening faster than normal
    D. closing unusually slowly

24. When a person signals for an elevator and the elevator skips his floor because it is already overcrowded, which of the following should automatically occur?
The

    A. elevator completes discharging passengers and returns to pick up the call
    B. signal is transferred to the next available car
    C. starter dispatches another car to answer the call
    D. signal puts more elevators into service

24.____

25. The MAIN reason that an elevator starter should watch the loading of the elevators is to insure that

    A. passengers will enter the cars quickly
    B. the number of passengers entering the car does not exceed the number allowed
    C. complaints from the passengers can be heard
    D. the public will see the need for elevator starters

25.____

KEY (CORRECT ANSWERS)

1. C		11. B
2. B		12. B
3. A		13. A
4. B		14. A
5. A		15. C
6. C		16. A
7. A		17. A
8. A		18. A
9. D		19. B
10. B		20. A

21. C
22. B
23. A
24. B
25. B

TEST 2

DIRECTIONS: Each question or incomplete statement is followed by several suggested answers or completions. Select the one that BEST answers the question or completes the statement. *PRINT THE LETTER OF THE CORRECT ANSWER IN THE SPACE AT THE RIGHT.*

1. Assume that an elevator is stuck and an elevator starter has spoken with the passengers on the intercom in order to reassure them.
   Of the following, the BEST action for the starter to take *next* is to

   A. ask the passengers for their home telephone numbers
   B. call the elevator mechanic
   C. stand by to assist in the emergency
   D. notify offices in the building that some of their employees are stuck in the elevator

   1._____

2. Starters are instructed never to allow an elevator to be moved that is not functioning properly.
   The MAIN reason for this is to

   A. avoid vandalism
   B. make the passengers comfortable
   C. prevent accidents
   D. simplify the repairs to be made

   2._____

3. After a starter has opened the shaft door of a manually operating elevator to place the car into service, the NEXT action that he should take is to

   A. put the lights on
   B. start the generator
   C. check to see that the floor is clean
   D. check that the car is at the landing

   3._____

4. Assume that an elevator starter sees a man trip and fall down near the elevators on the main floor of the building. The starter immediately goes over to the man, who says that he has twisted his ankle and cannot get up.
   Of the following, the FIRST action the starter should take is to

   A. ignore the incident since it was not caused by the operation of the elevators
   B. assist the injured man to move to a quiet area on the main floor
   C. summon an ambulance and be prepared to direct the medical people to the injured man
   D. make out a detailed accident report

   4._____

5. Of the following, the BEST way for a starter to maintain safe conditions for both passengers and employees is to *always*

   A. wear his uniform
   B. look busy
   C. keep a good attendance record
   D. observe rules and regulations

   5._____

6. A starter sees a man who is holding a typewriter run from an elevator and out of the building.
   The MOST important thing for the starter to try to remember right after the incident is

   A. the date of the incident
   B. the make or brand of the typewriter
   C. which elevator car the man was riding
   D. what the man looked like

7. In most buildings, it is requested that mail bags be carried out of the elevators instead of being dragged out. Of the following, the BEST reason for this is to

   A. prevent damage to the floor
   B. prevent damage to car panels
   C. make sure that the mail bags do not take up too much room in the elevators
   D. make the mailmen move faster

8. Assume that the only elevator in a building is being repaired and has been shut down by the mechanic during his lunch hour. A commissioner comes in and wants to go up to his office quickly.
   The BEST thing for a starter to do in this situation is to

   A. open the elevator and take the commissioner to his office
   B. tell the commissioner that a second elevator should be installed
   C. tell the commissioner that the elevator is out of service and tell him that he can use the stairs
   D. call the mechanic's supervisor and ask if it is all right to take the commissioner to his office

9. A starter observes a passenger leaving an elevator car with an open container of coffee. The passenger spills some coffee in front of the car landing on the main floor. The starter should IMMEDIATELY

   A. look for a porter
   B. report it to the custodian
   C. clean it up himself
   D. shut the cars down

10. The rated capacity of an elevator is usually stated in terms of

    A. velocity   B. horsepower
    C. acceleration   D. pounds

11. A starter notices a boy defacing the marble walls in the main floor lobby entrance of a building.
    Of the following, the FIRST action the starter should take is to

    A. ignore the boy's actions
    B. report the incident to the custodian
    C. force the boy to clean it up
    D. ask the boy to stop

12. Of the following, the MOST important reason for a starter to plan work schedules for the elevator operators under his supervision is so that   12._____

    A. unexpected emergency situations can be properly handled
    B. essential operations will be adequately covered
    C. the operators will be satisfied that the work is spread out equally
    D. the operators will know their jobs better

13. New instructions concerning the operation of a freight car were given to an elevator starter by his supervisor. If the starter does not understand these instructions, he should   13._____

    A. ask his supervisor to explain the new instructions
    B. follow the old procedures in the operation of the freight car
    C. ask the operator of the freight elevator for assistance
    D. have the regular freight operator brief him on the operations

14. A passenger complains that the elevator door hit him lightly on closing.
    The BEST thing for the elevator starter to do is to   14._____

    A. ask the passenger to report the incident to the custodian
    B. tell the passenger not to hold the door open for such a long time
    C. check the door and the safety light ray to see that they are working properly
    D. take the elevator out of service

15. The MOST important reason for a starter to remove dirt from the door floor saddle slot is to   15._____

    A. prevent the doors from becoming dirty
    B. allow the doors to close properly
    C. prevent the doors from being damaged
    D. make the porters' jobs easier

16. An elevator operator was injured as a result of slipping on an oily floor.
    This type of accident was MOST likely caused by   16._____

    A. defective equipment
    B. the physical condition of the operator
    C. improperly installed flooring
    D. poor housekeeping

17. If a car is stuck and there are no passengers in the elevator, which of the following is TRUE?
    The   17._____

    A. car will automatically return to service
    B. car door will automatically open
    C. starter will not have to report the incident
    D. alarm bell will not ring

18. Which of the following is NOT a duty of an elevator starter?   18._____

    A. Answering inquiries made by the public
    B. Observing the performance of a new elevator operator

C. Guarding against potential hazards
D. Delivering personal messages

19. A starter should be familiar with the location and main functions of agencies in the building MAINLY because this would

    A. show the public that the starter knows the job
    B. help the starter in directing persons to the right offices
    C. show that the starter is well educated
    D. increase the use of the elevators

20. The MAIN reason for quickly having the lights fixed when they go out in an elevator is to

    A. save power
    B. avoid accidents
    C. make dust visible
    D. restore the current

21. A woman tells an elevator starter that she is having difficulty completing an application for a certain city program whose office is located in the building. The woman asks the starter to help her complete the application.
    Which of the following is the BEST action for the starter to take?

    A. Help the woman complete the application and at the same time continue to perform his regular duties
    B. Tell the woman to complete the form as best she can
    C. Direct the woman to the program's office in the building
    D. Tell the woman that it would be illegal to help her

22. Of the following, the situation in which an elevator starter would be MOST justified in calling the police is if a passenger

    A. argues loudly with another passenger
    B. refuses to enter an elevator
    C. uses physical force on another passenger
    D. insults the starter

23. Elevator starters are urged to be courteous to passengers MAINLY because courtesy helps to

    A. maintain elevator schedules
    B. prevent unexpected accidents from occurring
    C. promote good public relations
    D. increase the use of elevators

24. In making a written report of an accident in which someone was injured, which of the following items is it LEAST important for an elevator starter to include in the report?

    A. The location of the accident
    B. An opinion of the extent of the injury
    C. The name of the injured person
    D. The date of the accident

25. Of the following, the MOST important reason for having an elevator starter write a complete report of a passenger accident which occurred in an elevator is to

    A. prove that the starter is alert
    B. assist in preventing future accidents
    C. assist the attending physician
    D. show that the elevator is safe

25._____

KEY (CORRECT ANSWERS)

1.	B		11.	D
2.	C		12.	B
3.	D		13.	A
4.	C		14.	C
5.	D		15.	B
6.	D		16.	D
7.	A		17.	D
8.	C		18.	D
9.	C		19.	B
10.	D		20.	B

21.	C
22.	C
23.	C
24.	B
25.	B

TEST 3

DIRECTIONS: Each question or incomplete statement is followed by several suggested answers or completions. Select the one that BEST answers the question or completes the statement. *PRINT THE LETTER OF THE CORRECT ANSWER IN THE SPACE AT THE RIGHT.*

Questions 1-6.

DIRECTIONS: Questions 1 through 6 are to be answered ONLY on the basis of the information given in the Elevator Operators' Work Schedule shown below.

ELEVATOR OPERATORS' WORK SCHEDULE

Operator	Hours of Work	A.M. Relief Period	Lunch Hour	P.M. Relief Period
Anderson	8:30-4:30	10:20-10:30	12:00- 1:00	2:20-2:30
Carter	8:00-4:00	10:10-10:20	11:45-12:45	2:30-2:40
Daniels	9:00-5:00	10:20-10:30	12:30- 1:30	3:15-3:25
Grand	9:30-5:30	11:30-11:40	1:00- 2:00	4:05-4:15
Jones	7:45-3:45	9:45- 9:55	11:30-12:30	2:05-2:15
Lewis	9:45-5:45	11:40-11:50	1:15- 2:15	4:20-4:30
Nance	8:45-4:45	10:50-11:00	12:30- 1:30	3:05-3:15
Perkins	8:00-4:00	10:00-10:10	12:00- 1:00	2:40-2:50
Russo	7:45-3:45	9:30- 9:40	11:30-12:30	2:10-2:20
Smith	9:45-5:45	11:45-11:55	1:15- 2:15	4:05-4:15

1. The two operators who are on P.M. relief at the same time are

   A. Anderson and Daniels   B. Carter and Perkins
   C. Jones and Russo   D. Grand and Smith

2. Of the following, the two operators who have the same lunch hour are

   A. Anderson and Perkins   B. Daniels and Russo
   C. Grand and Smith   D. Nance and Russo

3. At 12:15, the number of operators on their lunch hour is

   A. 3   B. 4   C. 5   D. 6

4. The operator who has an A.M. relief period right after Perkins and a P.M. relief period right before Perkins is

   A. Russo   B. Nance   C. Daniels   D. Carter

2 (#3)

5. The number of operators who are scheduled to be working at 4:40 is   5._____

    A. 5   B. 6   C. 7   D. 8

6. According to the schedule, it is MOST correct to say that   6._____

    A. no operator has a relief period during the time that another operator has a lunch hour
    B. each operator has to wait an identical amount of time between the end of lunch and the beginning of P.M. relief period
    C. no operator has a relief period before 9:45 or after 4:00
    D. each operator is allowed a total of 1 hour and 20 minutes for lunch hour and relief periods

7. In which of the following situations concerning an elevator operator is it MOST important for the operator's supervisor, an elevator starter, to take immediate action? The operator('s)   7._____

    A. uniform is not clean
    B. closes the car doors before the elevator is loaded to capacity
    C. answers an inquiry made by one of the passengers
    D. ignores a safety rule

8. Of the following, the BEST way for an elevator starter to make sure that elevator operators are performing their duties *properly* is to   8._____

    A. check the condition of the elevators daily
    B. ask the operators to follow instructions
    C. order one operator to report any errors committed by the other operators
    D. observe the operators at work and see how well they function

9. Which of the following should be the FIRST step in training a newly-hired elevator operator?   9._____

    A. Correct the operator's errors
    B. Show the operator how to do the work
    C. Write a report describing the operator's performance
    D. Let the operator do the job himself

10. In an emergency situation, an elevator starter should speak _____ manner.   10._____

    A. in a hurried and tense
    B. clearly and in a calm
    C. slowly and in a rambling
    D. quickly and in an excited

11. Of the following, which is the BEST way for a starter to instruct operators in the use of a new procedure?   11._____

    A. Tell one operator to show the other operators how to follow the new procedure
    B. Pass around a description of the new procedure
    C. Explain and demonstrate the new procedure to the operators
    D. Post a description of the new procedure on a bulletin board

12. When training new employees, a supervisor should expect that they will

    A. not all learn at the same rate
    B. need less training than experienced employees
    C. learn faster if the supervisor does not observe them performing their work
    D. learn better if they are trained during lunch hours

13. When introducing a new elevator operator to the job, an elevator starter should

    A. tell the operator that the work is very difficult
    B. have the operator memorize all the job's duties and responsibilities before beginning work
    C. tell the operator that every mistake will be noted on the probation report
    D. assume that the operator wants to perform as well as possible

14. An elevator operator tells her supervisor, an elevator starter, that she is considering submitting a suggestion to the employee suggestion program. The operator's suggestion concerns a way of improving elevator service in the building and may require the starter to occasionally walk greater distances than at present.
    Of the following, the BEST thing for the starter to do is to

    A. ask the operator whether she would like to walk around more if she were to become a starter
    B. encourage the operator to submit her idea to the employee suggestion program
    C. ask the operator to omit the part which requires the starter to do more work before submitting the suggestion
    D. tell the operator that employee suggestions are usually ignored

15. Assume that the elevator operators in a certain building have submitted their choices for vacation periods.
    In making up a vacation schedule for these operators, it would be MOST desirable for an elevator starter to

    A. try to give the operators their first choices for vacation periods
    B. make sure that the best operators get their first choice before preparing the rest of the schedule
    C. draw up a schedule first and then see how it compares with the operators' choices
    D. assign earlier vacation periods to senior operators and later periods to newer operators

16. In planning the daily work schedules for the elevator operators in a building, it would be MOST desirable for an elevator starter to

    A. give all the operators the same lunch hour so that they will eat together
    B. give longer rest periods to operators who have more seniority
    C. make sure that there are enough operators on duty during periods of heavy traffic
    D. assign the least desirable working hours to the newer operators

17. Of the following, the FIRST time an elevator starter should tell a new elevator operator the basic safety rules of the job is

    A. during the operator's introduction to the job
    B. once passengers have complained about the operator's recklessness

C. after the operator has had a minor accident when operating the elevators
D. when the operator completes the probation period

18. Assume that a newly hired elevator operator has been operating an elevator for two weeks.
    Of the following, which is the BEST method for the operator's supervisor, an elevator starter, to use thereafter in order to correct any mistakes which the operator makes?

    A. Draw up a weekly list of the operator's mistakes and discuss the list with the operator at the end of each week
    B. Wait until the operator makes the same mistake twice before correcting it
    C. Discuss each of the operator's mistakes together with the other operators so that they will be helped also
    D. Explain the proper procedure to the operator as soon as possible after a mistake is made

18.____

19. Assume that a certain elevator starter is at work 8 hours a day, which includes 1 hour for lunch and two 15-minute relief periods. The rest of the workday the starter is performing his duties.
    If the starter works 4 days, the TOTAL amount of time the starter will actually be performing his duties is _____ hours.

    A. 24   B. 26   C. 28   D. 32

19.____

20. Assume that a certain bank of 18 elevators operating at full capacity could move 3,240 passengers an hour from the main lobby.
    The number of passengers that one of these elevators could move from the lobby every 15 minutes is, on the average,

    A. 12   B. 22   C. 45   D. 180

20.____

21. In a certain agency, the amount of absence due to injury or illness was an average of 6 hours a month for each employee.
    If this agency had 335 employees, the TOTAL number of hours lost in a year due to injury or sickness was

    A. 4,020   B. 20,100   C. 24,120   D. 28,140

21.____

22. Assume that in a certain building the elevators must handle 16% of the building population during a peak traffic period.
    If the building population is 2,825, the TOTAL number of people the elevators must handle during a peak traffic period is

    A. 396   B. 424   C. 436   D. 452

22.____

Questions 23-26

DIRECTIONS: Questions 23 through 26 are to be answered ONLY on the basis of the information given in the paragraph below.

The speed at which an elevator should run depends upon several considerations: the height of the building, the size of the building, the purpose for which the elevator will be used, and how the elevator will be used. Elevators with extremely high speeds are of little advantage unless an express run can be established to make use of it. On local runs, by the time an elevator accelerates and then decelerates for landing, there is little time to take advantage of speed. It should also be noted that the higher the elevator speed, the larger the machine, and hence the greater the cost. Therefore, the situation must be studied before each installation and the proper speed selected to avoid the purchase of unnecessary equipment.

23. According to the above paragraph, extremely high-speed elevators are of little advantage unless 23.____

    A. the building is small
    B. there are only two elevators in a large building
    C. they are used on express runs
    D. they accelerate and decelerate slowly on local runs

24. Which one of the following is NOT mentioned in the above paragraph as a consideration in selecting the speed at which an elevator should run? 24.____

    A. Height of the building   B. Age of the building
    C. Size of the building   D. Purpose of the elevator

25. Based on the paragraph, it would be MOST correct to say that a high-speed elevator _____ than a low-speed elevator. 25.____

    A. accelerates more slowly   B. uses less equipment
    C. breaks down more often   D. costs more

26. According to the above paragraph, one of the ways to avoid the purchase of unnecessary elevator equipment is to 26.____

    A. study the situation before each installation
    B. buy only low-speed elevators
    C. use smaller machines for high-speed elevators
    D. select low-speed elevators for express runs

Questions 27-30.

DIRECTIONS: Questions 27 through 30 are to be answered ONLY on the basis of the information given in the paragraph below.

Careful planning should always be given to the grouping of elevators in a building. When more than one elevator serves a building, the elevators should be located together as a single group or series of groups. Individual groups should be so arranged that the walking distance from the landing button to the furthermost elevator is kept at a minimum. The *alcove* arrangement, preferred for groups of five through eight elevators, has the advantage of preventing interference between people waiting for the elevators and people passing through the main corridor. It also holds *walking distance* to a minimum. The *straight line* arrangement is satisfactory for up to five cars. More than that will result in serious delays in service since the elevators must frequently wait while passengers walk from the extremities of the group.

27. According to the above paragraph, one way to prevent interference between people waiting for elevators and people using the main corridor is to 27.____

    A. use the *straight line* arrangement of elevators
    B. use the *alcove* arrangement of elevators

C. place the landing button next to the elevator farthest from the main corridor
D. eliminate the access from the main corridor to the elevator

28. According to the above paragraph, serious delays in elevator service may be caused by   28.____

    A. locating elevators together as a group or series of groups
    B. keeping *walking distance* to a minimum
    C. having six elevator cars in an *alcove* arrangement
    D. having seven elevator cars in a *straight line* arrangement

29. Based on the above paragraph, which of the following is the MOST accurate statement concerning the grouping of elevators in a building?   29.____

    A. The grouping of elevators always requires careful planning.
    B. Elevators should always be grouped in an *alcove* arrangement.
    C. Elevators should always be grouped in a *straight line* arrangement.
    D. A building should never contain more than eight elevators.

30. Based on the information given in the paragraph, which of the following is a preferred way of arranging twelve elevator cars in a building?   30.____

    A. All twelve cars in one *alcove*
    B. All twelve cars in a *straight line*
    C. Four cars in one *alcove* and eight cars in a *straight line*
    D. Six cars in each of two *alcoves*

KEY (CORRECT ANSWERS)

1. D	11. C	21. C
2. A	12. A	22. D
3. C	13. D	23. C
4. D	14. B	24. B
5. A	15. A	25. D
6. D	16. C	26. A
7. D	17. A	27. B
8. D	18. D	28. D
9. B	19. B	29. A
10. B	20. C	30. D

ELEVATOR MECHANICS

EXAMINATION SECTION
TEST 1

DIRECTIONS: Each question, or incomplete statement is followed by several suggested answers or completions. Select the one that BEST answers the question or completes the statement. PRINT THE LETTER OF THE CORRECT ANSWER IN THE SPACE AT THE RIGHT.

Questions 1-16.

DIRECTIONS: Questions 1 to 16 refer to the tools shown on page 2. (The numbers in the answer refer to the numbers beneath the tools. Tools are NOT drawn to scale.)

1. A 1" x 1" x 1/8" angle iron should be cut by using tool number   1._____
   A. A, 7   B. B, 12   C. 23   D. 42

2. To peen an iron rivet, you should use tool number   2._____
   A. 4   B. 7   C. 21   D. 43

3. The "star drill" is tool number   3._____
   A. 5.   B. 10   C. 20   D. 22

4. To make holes in sheet metal for sheet metal screws, you should use tool number   4._____
   A. 6   B. 10   C. 36   D. D, 46

5. To cut through a 3/8" diameter wire rope, you should use tool number   5._____
   A. 12   B. 23   C. 42   D. 54

6. To remove cutting burrs from the inside of a steel pipe, you should use tool number   6._____
   A. 5   B. 11   C. 14   D. 20

7. The depth of a bored hole may be measured most accurately with tool number   7._____
   A. 8   B. 16   C. 26   D. 41

8. If the marking on the blade of tool number 7 reads: "12-32," the 32 refers to the   8._____
   A. length   B. thickness
   C. weight   D. no. of teeth per inch

9. If tool number 6 bears the mark "5," it should be used to drill holes having a diameter of   9._____
   A. 5/32"   B. 5/16"   C. 5/8"   D. 5"

10. To determine most quickly the number of threads per inch on a bolt, you should use tool number   10._____
    A. 8   B. 16   C. 26   D. 50

37

11. Wood screws, located in positions where the headroom does not permit the use of an ordinary screwdriver, may be removed by using tool number 11.____

   A. 17 B. 28 C. 35 D. 46

12. To remove a broken-off piece of 1/2" diameter pipe from a fitting, you should use tool number 12.____

   A. 5 B. 11 C. 20 D. D, 36

13. The outside diameter of a bushing may be measured *most accurately* with tool number 13.____

   A. 8 B. 26 C. 33 D. 43

14. To rethread a stud hole in the casting of an elevator motor, you should use tool number 14.____

   A. 5 B. 20 C. 22 D. 36

3 (#1)

TOOLS

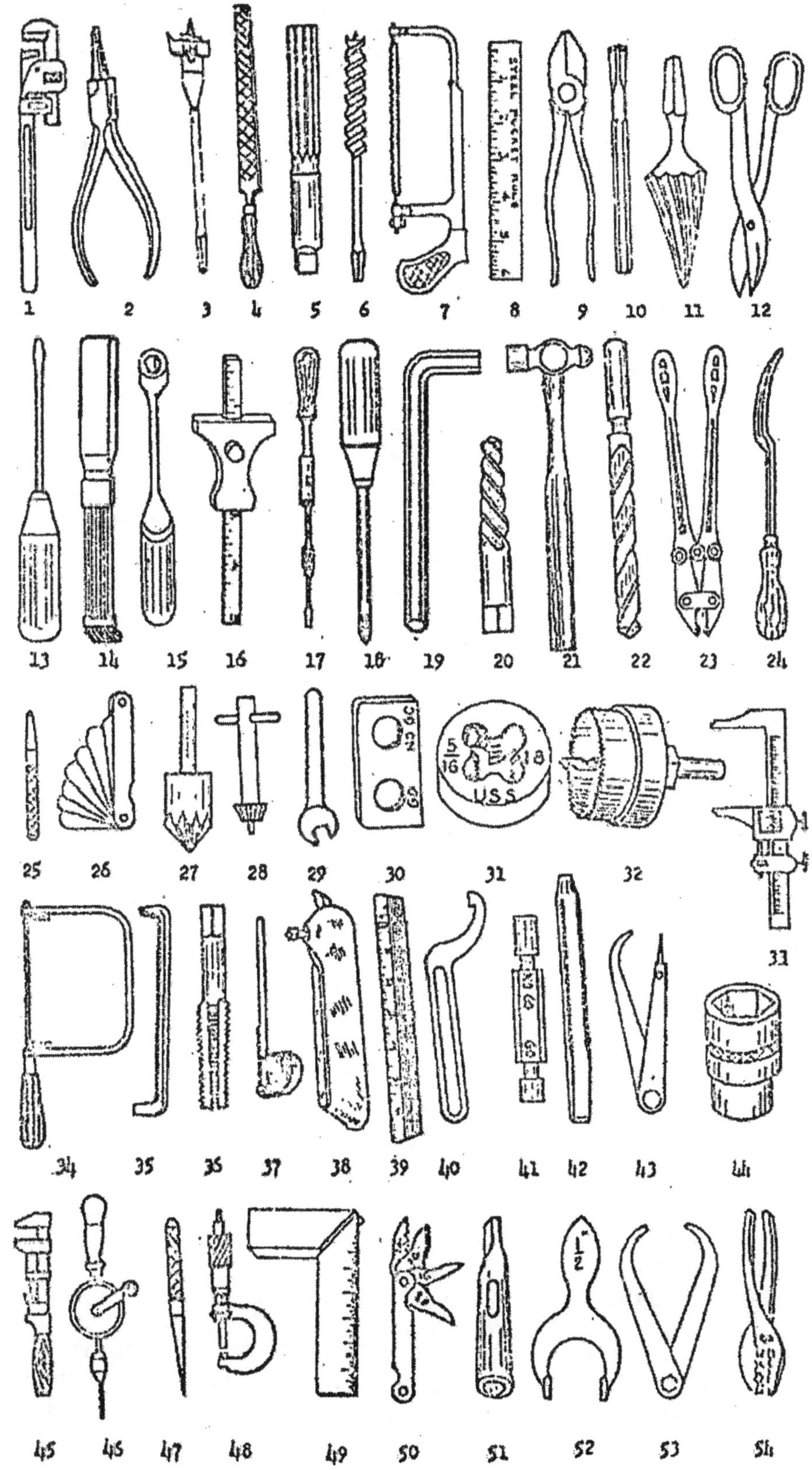
1 2 3 4 5 6 7 8 9 10 11 12
STEEL POCKET RULE
13 14 15 16 17 18 19 20 21 22 23 24
5/16
18
USS
25 26 27 28 29 30 31 32
33
34 35 35 37 38 39 40 41 42 43 44
45 45 47 48 49 50 51 52 53 54

15. To enlarge *slightly* a bored hole in a steel plate, you should use tool number 15.____

    A. 5   B. 11   C. 20   D. D, 36

16. The term "16-oz." should be applied to tool number 16.____

    A. 1   B. 12   C. 21   D. 42

Questions 17-19.

DIRECTIONS: Questions 17 to 19 refer to the carbon resistor sketched below. Refer to this sketch when answering these questions.

17. Color coding is used on the resistor rather than having its rating printed on it MAINLY because the 17.____

    A. printing would fade in time
    B. color coding is simple to remember
    C. color coding prevents mix-ups
    D. resistor is too small for printing

18. Band number 3 on the resistor indicates the 18.____

    A. decimal multiplier
    B. third significant figure
    C. voltage rating
    D. percent tolerance

19. If band number 4 is missing from the resistor, it means that the resistor"s 19.____

    A. voltage is doubled
    B. voltage is zero
    C. tolerance is zero
    D. tolerance is 20 percent

20. The wire rope used for elevator hoisting consists of a number of wires laid into a strand, and a number of strands laid around a rope center. If the wires are laid left-handed into the strands, and the strands are laid right-handed around the rope center, the rope is called a 20.____

A. right-lay, regular-lay rope
B. left-lay, regular-lay rope
C. right-lay, Lang-lay rope
D. left-lay, Lang-lay rope

21. A *megger* should be used for the direct measurement of 21._____

   A. current   B. power   C. voltage   D. resistance

22. It is considered *bad* practice to use water to put out electrical fires *MAINLY* because the water may 22._____

   A. short-circuit the wires
   B. damage the insulation
   C. rust delicate equipment
   D. cause a serious electrical shock

23. Of the following, the method that should *NOT* be used to remove a length of hoist rope from its delivery reel is: 23._____

   A. Take off the rope from the top side while the reel is resting on its side
   B. Fix the free end and then roll the reel along the floor
   C. Mount the reel on a shaft and trunnions and then rotate the reel
   D. Mount the reel on a turntable and then rotate the turntable

24. The area of a circle, whose diameter is 24 inches, is, most nearly, 24._____

   A. 0.84 square foot
   B. 1.67 square feet
   C. 3.14 square feet
   D. 18.84 square feet

25. If an elevator mechanic opens the strands of a piece of manila rope and finds saw-dust material inside the rope, he should know that this means that the rope 25._____

   A. is relatively new
   B. has been damaged and should be discarded
   C. has dried out and must be re-oiled before use
   D. is to be used only for lights loads until the sawdust works itself out

26. Elevator mechanics are cautioned not to leave tools on scaffolding. The *MOST* important reason for this rule is to 26._____

   A. avoid a safety hazard
   B. prevent damage to the tools
   C. prevent theft of the tools
   D. prevent mix-ups in the mechanics' tools

Questions 27-40.

DIRECTIONS: Questions 27 to 40 are based on the sketch of a gearless elevator shown on page 6.

27. The *governor* is indicated by number   27.____
    A. 2   B. 7   C. 8   D. 16

28. The *motor generator* is indicated by number   28.____
    A. 1   B. 4   C. 7   D. 9

29. The *floor selector* is indicated by number   29.____
    A. 1   B. 2   C. 11   D. 16

30. The *hoistway limit switch* is indicated by number   30.____
    A. 8   B. 9   C. 10   D. 12

31. The *cable equalizer* is indicated by number   31.____
    A. 8   B. 9   C. 14   D. 26

32. The *brakes* are indicated by number   32.____
    A. 2   B. 5   C. 9   D. 22

33. The *buffers* are indicated by number   33.____
    A. 3   B. 9   C. 24   D. 25

34. The *compensating rope sheave* is indicated by number   34.____
    A. 8   B. 9   C. 25   D. 26

35. The *deflector sheave* is indicated by number   35.____
    A. 8   B. 9   C. 25   D. 26

36. The *door engines* are indicated by number   36.____
    A. 11   B. 12   C. 15   D. 16

37. The *guide shoes* are indicated by number   37.____
    A. 11   B. 12   C. 16   D. 20

38. The *music box* is indicated by number   38.____
    A. 3   B. 7   C. 11   D. 16

39. The *releasing carrier* is indicated by number   39.____
    A. 14   B. 16   C. 22   D. 27

40. The *rail grip shoes* are indicated by number   40.____
    A. 5   B. 17   C. 25   D. 26

7 (#1)

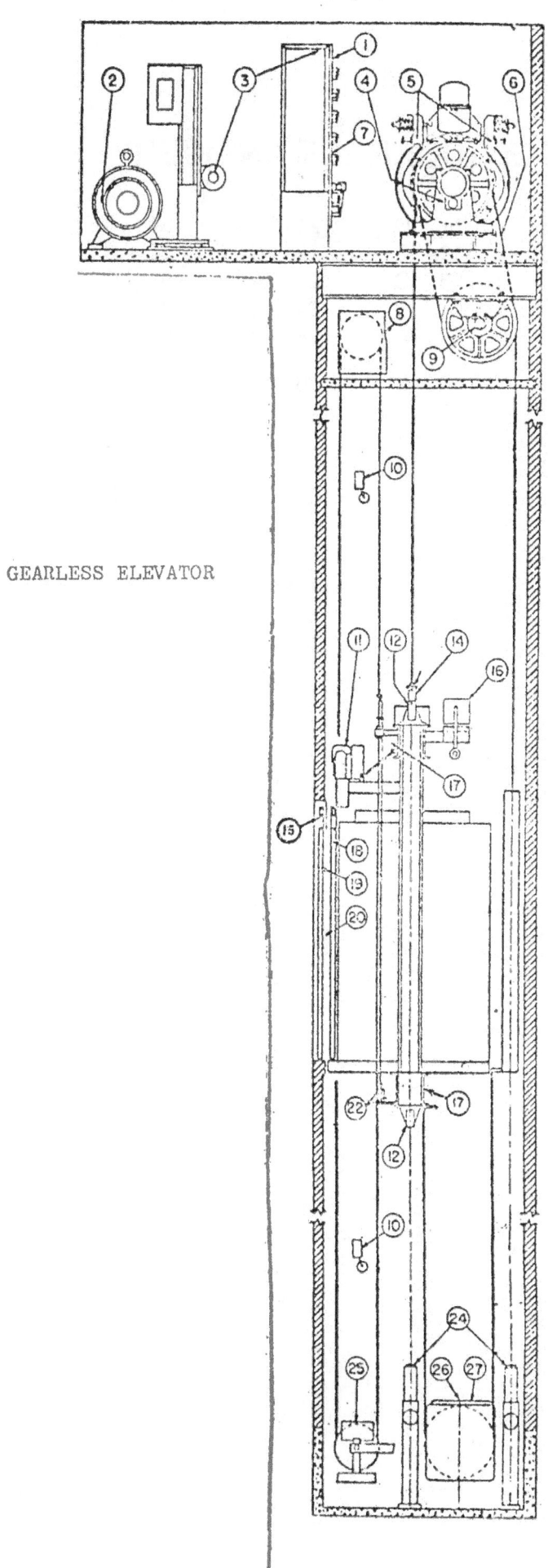

GEARLESS ELEVATOR

43

KEY(CORRECT ANSWER)

1. A	11. C	21. D	31. C
2. C	12. C	22. D	32. B
3. B	13. C	23. A	33. C
4. D	14. D	24. C	34. D
5. B	15. A	25. B	35. B
6. B	16. C	26. A	36. A
7. B	17. D	27. C	37. B
8. D	18. A	28. A	38. D
9. B	19. D	29. A	39. C
10. D	20. A	30. C	40. B

TEST 2

Questions 1-5.

DIRECTIONS: For Questions 1 to 5, the item referred to is shown to the right of the question.

1. The sketch shows a method of preventing a manila rope from unraveling. This is called
   A. splicing
   B. seizing
   C. mousing
   D. whipping

2. The placing of a rope yarn on a hook to prevent the chain from being accidentally detached, as shown in the sketch, is called
   A. mousing
   B. whipping
   C. splicing
   D. seizing

3. The knot shown is called a
   A. timber hitch
   B. clove hitch
   C. bowline
   D. becket

4. The rigging device shown is a
   A. screw clamp
   B. shackle
   C. clevis
   D. thimble

5. The wire-rope clip shown is a
   A. Crosby
   B. Loughlin
   C. Fist-grip
   D. C-clamp

6. It is considered *good* practice to release the pressure from a hose containing compressed air before uncoupling the hose connection because this avoids

   A. damage to the air tool
   B. damage to the air compressor
   C. wasting compressed air
   D. possible personal injury

7. Of the following electrical circuit components, the *one* which may give you an electrical shock even after the electrical power is turned off is a(n)

   A. charged capacitor
   B. resistor
   C. interlock
   D. relay

Questions 8-14.

DIRECTIONS: For Questions 8 to 14, the item referred to is shown to the right of the question.

8. If the upper fuse is good and the lower fuse is burnt out, the test lamp that should be on is number
   A. 1
   B. 2
   C. 3
   D. 4

9. If the 1.5V battery has an internal resistance of 0.1 ohm and the 0.8V battery has an internal resistance of 0.3 ohm, then the current in the circuit is, most nearly,
   A. 0.2 amperes
   B. 1.8 amperes
   C. 4.2 amperes
   D. 17.5 amperes

10. If the 10-ohm resistor, marked X, burns out, the voltmeter reading will become, most nearly,
    A. 0
    B. 20
    C. 80
    D. 100

11. The total resistance in the circuit is, most nearly,
    A. 1.7 ohms
    B. 4.5 ohms
    C. 14 ohms
    D. 21 ohms

12. The power used by the heater is
    A. 120 watts
    B. 720 watts
    C. 2400 watts
    D. 4320 watts

13. If two amperes flow through the circuit, the terminal voltages is
    A. 2 volts
    B. 6 volts
    C. 12 volts
    D. 24 volts

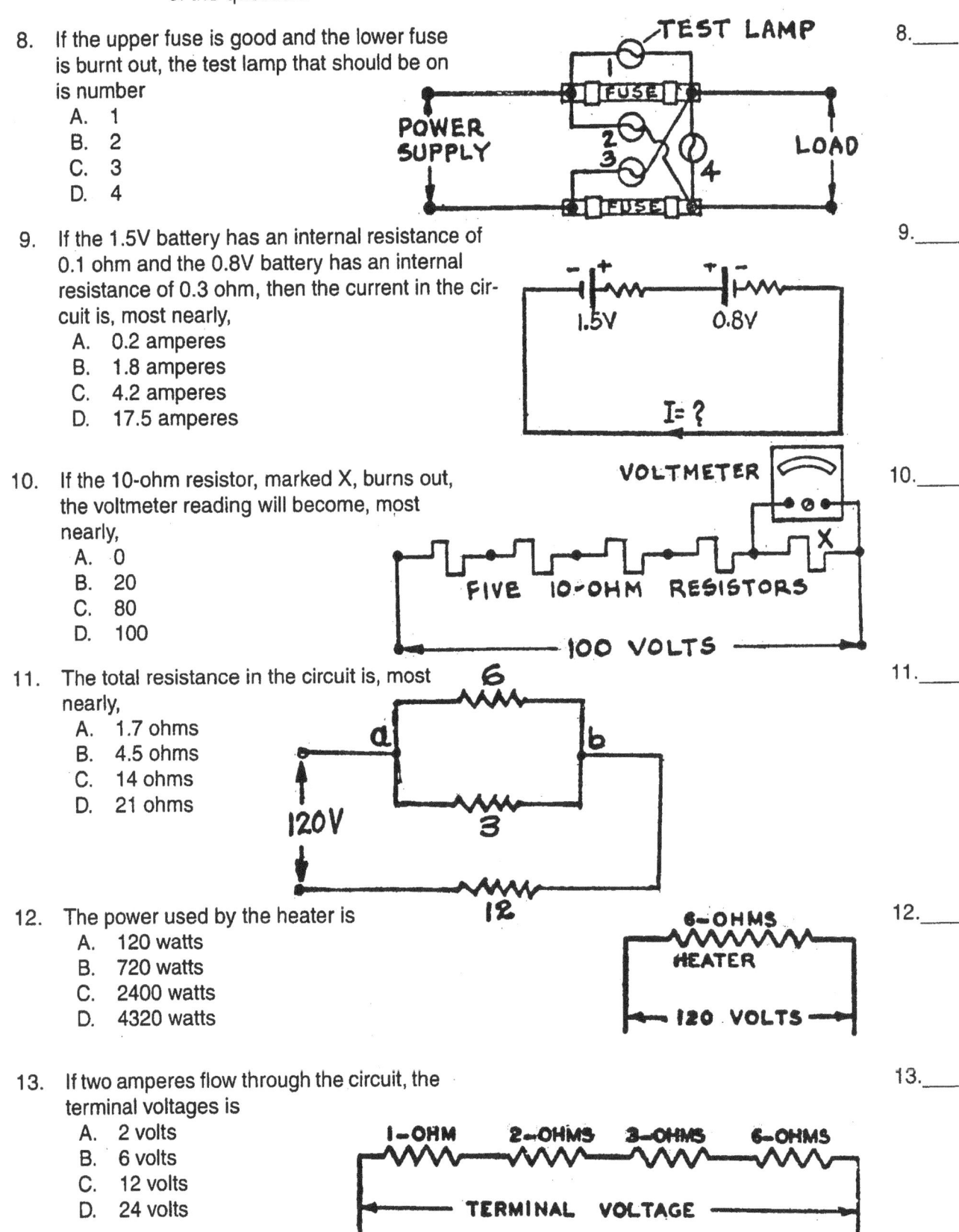

3 (#2)

14. If the two voltmeters are identical, and the battery voltage is 120 volts, then the readings of the voltmeters should be
    A. 60 volts on each meter
    B. 120 volts on each meter
    C. 120 volts on meter #1, 240 volts on meter #2
    D. 120 volts on meter #1, zero volts on meter #2

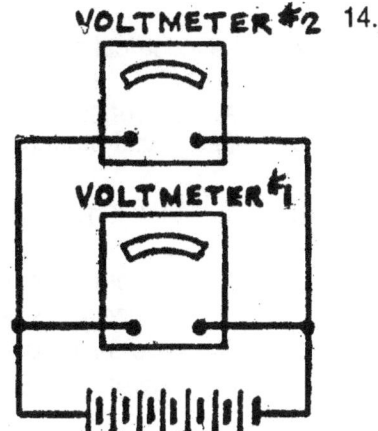

Questions 15-25.

DIRECTIONS: Questions 15 to 25 refer to the ELEVATOR WIRING DIAGRAM shown below. Refer to this diagram when answering these questions.

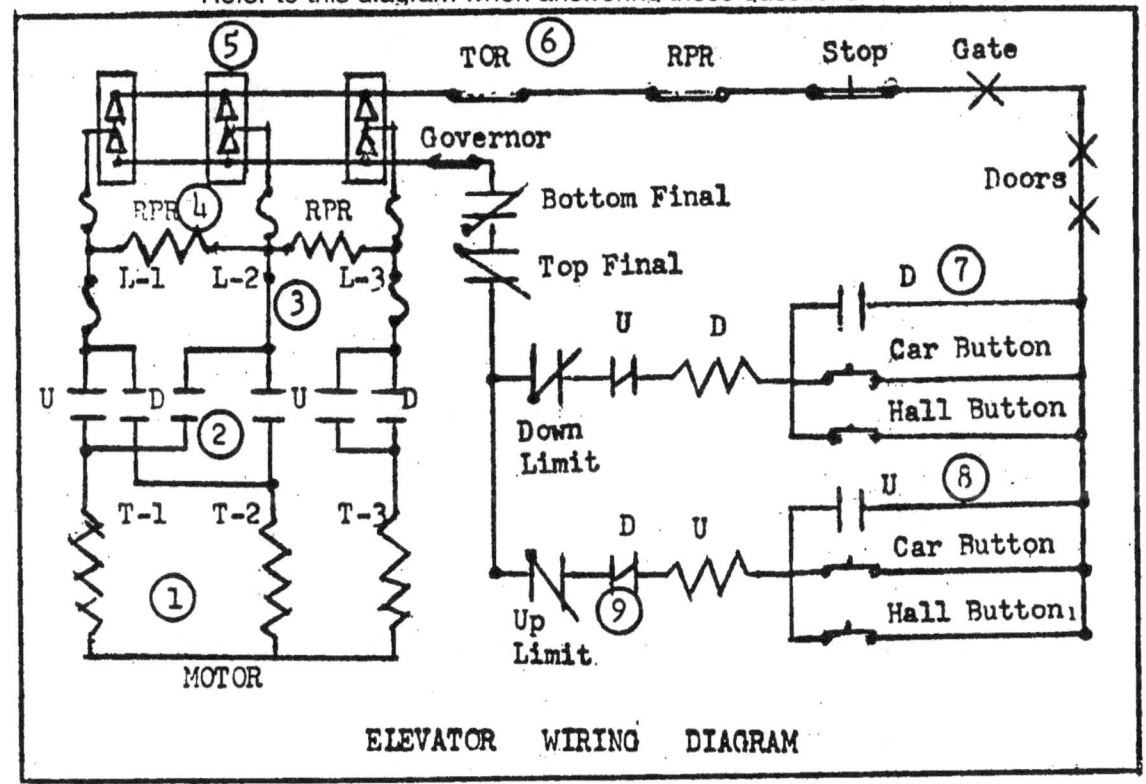

15. The electrical symbol motor's ⟋⟍⟋⟍ at ① indicates the motor's

    A. field windings
    B. electrical interlocks
    C. starting coil
    D. relay

16. The *MAIN* function of the wiring of L-l and L-2 through the U and D contactors at ② is to

    A. prevent overloading oiH;he motor
    B. permit reversing the motor
    C. prevent sharing the load between T-l, T-2
    D. permit different voltages to be applied

4 (#2)

17. The electrical symbols L-l, L-2 and L-3 at ③ indicate the

   A. power supply
   B. motor current
   C. circuit breakers
   D. line resistance

17.____

18. The *MAIN* function of the electrical component, labelled RPR at ④ is to

   A. prevent voltage changes in the circuit
   B. reduce the amount of current through the motor
   C. reverse the phases of the motor as the direction changes
   D. prevent elevator operation in case of reversa of the power supply phase

18.____

19. The *MAIN* function of the rectifiers at ⑤ is to

   A. reduce the voltage
   B. increase the current
   C. change A.C. to D.C.
   D. prevent current reversal

19.____

20. The *MAIN* function of the electrical component, labelled TOR at ⑥ is to

   A. prevent overspeeding
   B. cut in at terminal floor
   C. cut out at excessive torque
   D. prevent overheating

20.____

21. The arrangement of this circuit which prevents both the D contactor at ⑦ and the U contactor at ⑧ from being energized at the same time, is called a(n)

   A. interlock
   B. by-pass connection
   C. cross connection
   D. override

21.____

22. The pressing of the top-floor hall button while the car is descending will *NOT* prevent the elevator car from continuing downward because the

   A. down limit is closed
   B. D contact at ⑨ is opened
   C. down limit is opened
   D. D contact at ⑨ is closed

22.____

23. If the elevator car overspeeds, the safety device that should operate *first* is the

   A. Governor   B. Top final   C. Up limit   D. Stop

23.____

24. The *MAIN* function of the "Up Limit' and the "Down Limit" switch is to

   A. prevent the elevator car from hitting either pit or overhead

24.____

B. stop the elevator car nearly level with the landing
C. prevent the counterweight from hitting either at the top or bottom
D. keep the car speed within limits on the up and down trips

25. The "Bottom Final" and the "Top Final" switches are *usually* operated by   25.____

    A. the tiller rope   B. the selector tape
    C. cams   D. coils

26. It is considered *good* practice to lubricate elevator machinery   26.____

    A. during slack periods
    B. whenever it is needed
    C. at regularly scheduled times
    D. after a shut-down

27. Of the following, the *one* that should be used to dress a motor commutator is   27.____

    A. emery cloth   B. sandpaper
    C. a flat file   D. a mill file

28. A *tachometer* should be used for the direct measurement of   28.____

    A. torque   B. power factor
    C. specific gravity   D. r.p.m.

29. If 0.0375 is divided by 0.125, the result is   29.____

    A. 30.0   B. 3.0   C. 0.3   D. 0.03

30. It is considered *good* rigging practice to inspect chains more closely than wire rope prior to use MAINLY because chains   30.____

    A. twist more easily   B. stretch more
    C. rust more readily   D. have less reserve strength

31. A *hydrometer* should be used for the *direct* measurement of   31.____

    A. A torque   B. power factor
    C. r.p.m.   D. specific gravity

32. Of the following, elevator hoisting cables should be lubricated with   32.____

    A. a heavy grease   B. medium-heavy oil
    C. graphite   D. tar

33. If you were directed to check the 'backlash' on an elevator hoisting motor, you should check the   33.____

    A. gears   B. bearings   C. contactors   D. brakes

34. The MAIN function of a "pole shader" on a coil is to   34.____

    A. prevent heating   B. prevent hum
    C. reduce resistance   D. reduce flux

Questions 35-40.

DIRECTIONS: Questions 35 to 40 refer to the elevator CALL BUTTON CIRCUIT shown below. Refer to this circuit when answering these questions.

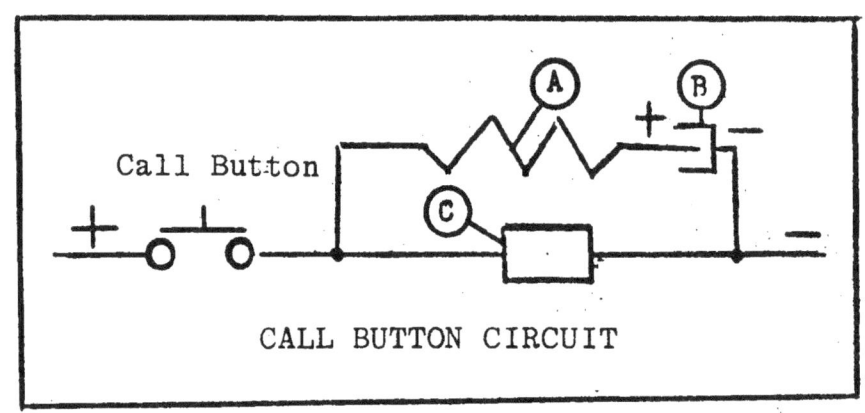

CALL BUTTON CIRCUIT

35. The electrical component shown at A is a   35.____

    A. resistor   B. coil   C. condenser   D. contactor

36. The electrical component shown at B is a   36.____

    A. resistor   B. coil   C. condenser   D. contactor

37. The electrical component shown at C is a   37.____

    A. resistor   B. coil   C. condenser   D. contactor

38. The *MAIN* purpose of component A is to   38.____

    A. short circuit B   B. limit current to B
    C. reduce voltage to C   D. increase current to C

39. The *MAIN* purpose of component B is to   39.____

    A. time the circuit
    B. increase the voltage
    C. decrease button resistance
    D. interrupt the circuit

40. The *MAIN* purpose of component C is to   40.____

    A. reduce the current
    B. increase the voltage
    C. open and close contactors
    D. reverse current polarity

KEY (CORRECT ANSWERS)

1. D	11. C	21. A	31. D
2. A	12. C	22. B	32. B
3. C	13. D	23. A	33. A
4. B	14. B	24. B	34. A
5. A	15. A	25. C	35. A
6. D	16. B	26. C	36. C
7. A	17. A	27. B	37. B
8. C	18. D	28. D	38. B
9. B	19. C	29. C	39. A
10. D	20. D	30. D	40. C

EXAMINATION SECTION
TEST 1

DIRECTIONS: Each question or incomplete statement is followed by several suggested answers or completions. Select the one that BEST answers the question or completes the statement. *PRINT THE LETTER OF THE CORRECT ANSWER IN THE SPACE AT THE RIGHT.*

1. Which of the following capacitors could be damaged by a reversal in polarity? A(n) _____ capacitor.

    A. ceramic   B. paper   C. mica
    D. electrolytic   E. vacuum

    1.____

2. If the current through a resistor is 6 amperes and the voltage drop across it is 100 volts, what is the approximate value of the resistor in ohm(s)?

    A. 1660   B. 166   C. 16.6   D. 1.66   E. 0.0166

    2.____

3. What is the CORRECT use for an arbor press?

    A. Bending sheet metal
    B. Driving self-tapping screws
    C. Removing screws
    D. Removing "C" rings
    E. Removing bearings from shafts

    3.____

4. Which one of the following is a tensioning device in bulk-belt-type conveyor systems?
    _____ take-up.

    A. Spring   B. Power   C. Hydraulic
    D. Fluid coupled   E. Flexible coupled

    4.____

5. When $X_L = X_C$ in a series circuit, what condition exists?

    A. The circuit impedance is increasing
    B. The circuit is at resonant frequency
    C. The circuit current is minimum
    D. The circuit has no e.m.f. at this time
    E. None of the above

    5.____

6. Which of the following pieces of information is NOT normally found on a schematic diagram?

    A. Functional stage name   B. Supply voltages
    C. Part symbols   D. Part values
    E. Physical location of parts

    6.____

7. When a single-phase induction motor drawing 24 amps at 120 VAC is reconnected to 240 VAC, what will be the amperage at 240 VAC? _____ amps.

    A. 6   B. 8   C. 12   D. 24   E. 36

    7.____

8. Which one of the following meters measures the SMALLEST current?   8._____

    A. Kilometer   B. Milliammeter   C. Microvoltmeter
    D. Millivoltmeter   E. Kilovoltmeter

9. If the current through a 1000-ohm resistor is 3 milliamperes, the voltage drop   9._____
   across the resistor is _____ volt(s).

    A. 1   B. 2.5   C. 3   D. 30   E. 300

10. The normally closed contacts of a relay are open when its solenoid is energized   10._____
    with VDC. The voltage at which the contacts re-close will be

    A. dependent upon the current through the contacts
    B. dependent upon the voltage applied to the contacts
    C. 24 VDC through the coil
    D. more than 24 VDC through the contacts
    E. less than 24 VDC through the coil

11. Electrical energy is converted to mechanical rotation by what component in the   11._____
    electric motor?

    A. Armature   B. Commutator   C. Field
    D. Start windings   E. Stator

12. Ohm's Law expresses the basic relationship of   12._____

    A. current, voltage, and resistance
    B. current, voltage, and power
    C. current, power, and resistance
    D. resistance, impedance, and voltage
    E. resistance, power, and impedance

13. In parallel circuits, the voltage is *always*   13._____

    A. variable   B. constant   C. alternating
    D. fluctuating   E. sporadic

14. Which one of the following is used as a voltage divider?   14._____

    A. Rotary converter   B. Potentiometer   C. Relay
    D. Circuit breaker   E. Voltmeter

Question 15.

Question 15 is based on the following diagram.

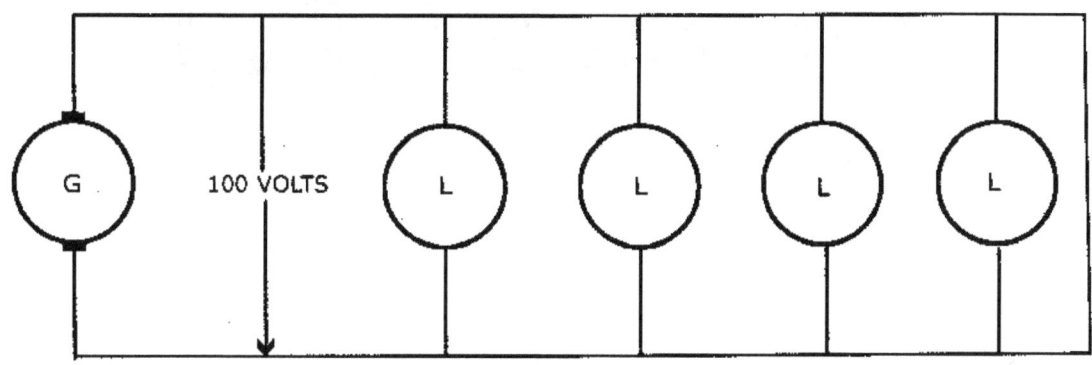

CURRENT IN EACH LAMP 1/2 AMPERE

15. What is the resistance of the entire circuit? _____ ohms.

   A. 15   B. 25   C. 35   D. 45   E. 50

16. Which one of the following tools is used to bring a bore to a specified tolerance?

   A. Tap
   D. Counterbore
   B. Reamer
   E. Center drill
   C. Countersink

17. The primary function of a take-up pulley in a belt conveyor is to

   A. carry the belt on the return trip
   B. track the belt
   C. maintain the proper belt tension
   D. change the direction of the belt
   E. regulate the speed of the belt

Question 18.

Question 18 is based on the following diagram.

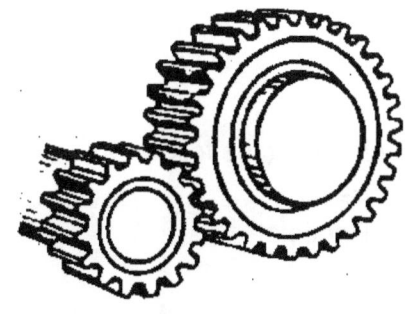

18. What is the name of the gears?

   A. Spur external
   D. Herringbone
   B. Spur internal
   D. Worm
   C. Helical

Question 19.

Question 19 is based on the following diagram.

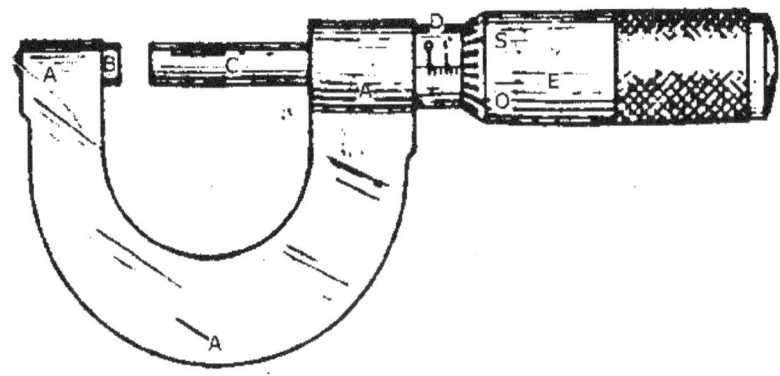

19. The part labeled D is the
    A. sleeve
    B. thimble
    C. frame
    D. anvil
    E. pindle

19.____

Question 20.

Question 20 is based on the following symbol.

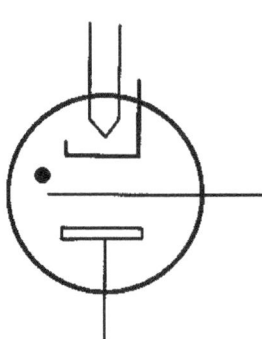

20. This symbol represents a _____ tube.
    A. thyratron vacuum
    B. thyratron gas
    C. variable-mu vacuum
    D. variable-mu gas
    E. vacuum photo

20.____

21. A diode can be substituted for which one of the following?
    A. Transformer
    B. Relay
    C. Rectifier
    D. Condenser
    E. Rheostat

21.____

Question 22.

Question 22 is based on the following diagram.

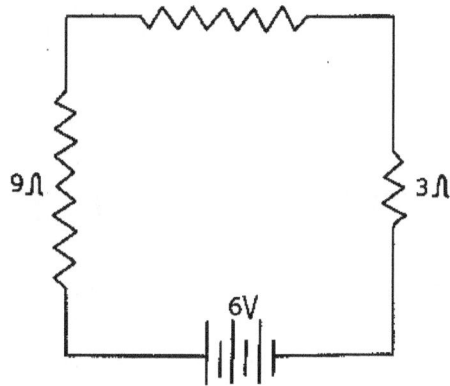

22. The rate of amperes flowing in the circuit is:

    A. .03 1/3 B. .18 C. .24
    D. .30 1/3 E. .33 1/3

23. The firing point in a thyratron tube is *most usually* controlled by the

    A. cathode B. grid C. plate
    D. heater   E. envelope

Questions 24-25.

Questions 24 and 25 shall be answered in accordance with the diagram below.

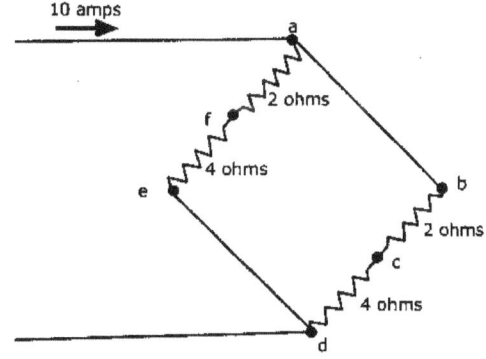

24. With reference to the above diagram, the voltage difference between points c and f is, *most nearly,* in volts,

    A. 40 B. 20 C. 10 D. 5 E. 0

25. With reference to the above diagram, the current flowing through the resistance c d is, *most nearly,* in amperes,

    A. 10 B. 5 C. 4 D. 2 E. 1

KEY (CORRECT ANSWERS)

1. D	6. E	11. A	16. B	21. C
2. C	7. C	12. A	17. C	22. E
3. E	8. B	13. B	18. A	23. B
4. A	9. C	14. B	19. A	24. E
5. B	10. E	15. E	20. B	25. B

EXAMINATION SECTION
TEST 1

DIRECTIONS: Each question or incomplete statement is followed by several suggested answers or completions. Select the one that BEST answers the question or completes the statement. *PRINT THE LETTER OF THE CORRECT ANSWER IN THE SPACE AT THE RIGHT.*

1. Two gears are meshed. The first gear has 20 teeth per inch and is rotating at 500 rpms. What is the speed of the second gear if it has 40 teeth per inch? _____ rpms.

   A. 500   B. 400   C. 250   D. 200

   1._____

2. With two meshed gears, the first gear rotates at 100 rpms, the second gear rotates at 2000 rpms and has 10 teeth per inch.
   The first gear has _____ number of teeth per inch.

   A. 200   B. 100   C. 50   D. 150

   2._____

3. Two pulleys are connected. The first pulley has a diameter of 5 inches; the second pulley has a diameter of 15 inches and rotates at 25 rpms.
   The speed of the first pulley is _____ rpms.

   A. 30   B. 75   C. 200   D. 400

   3._____

4. Of two connected pulleys, the first has a radius of 10 inches and rotates at 50 rpms; the second rotates at 25 rpms.
   The diameter of the second pulley is _____ inches.

   A. 40   B. 30   C. 20   D. 10

   4._____

5. Two pulleys are connected. The first pulley rotates at 75 rpms; the second pulley rotates at 100 rpms and has a diameter of 9 inches.
   The diameter of the first pulley is _____ inches.

   A. 10   B. 12   C. 15   D. 20

   5._____

6. Of two connected pulleys, the first pulley has a radius of 12 inches and rotates at 60 rpms; the second pulley has a diameter of 16 inches.
   The speed of the second pulley is _____ rpms.

   A. 1000   B. 1020   C. 1040   D. 1080

   6._____

7. If 16_{10} were converted to base 2, 8, and 16, the results would be _____ base 2, _____ base 8, and _____ base 16, respectively.

   A. 10000; 20; 10
   C. 20000; 200; 20
   B. 1000; 2000; 20
   D. 2000; 100; 10

   7._____

8. Converting CAF_{16} to base 10 and base 8, the results would be _____ base 10 and _____ base 8, respectively.

   A. 2437; 2567
   C. 4327; 5267
   B. 3247; 6257
   D. 3427; 2657

   8._____

2 (#1)

9. Converting 101011001_2 to base 8, 10, and 16, the results would be _____ base 8, _____ base 10, and _____ base 16, respectively.

   A. 135; 45; 59
   B. 567; 435; 259
   C. 315; 245; 135
   D. 531; 345; 159

   9.____

10. If 136_8 were converted to base 2, 10, and 16, the results would be _____ base 2, _____ base 10, and _____ base 16, respectively.

    A. 001011110; 94, 5E
    B. 010100110; 92; 10E
    C. 00100000; 90; 15E
    D. 011001110; 96; 20E

    10.____

11. It may be correctly stated that 1000 picofarads are equal to _____ microfarads.

    A. .0001   B. .001   C. .01   D. .1

    11.____

12. If 5 megohms were converted to kohms, the result would be _____ kohms.

    A. 1000   B. 2000   C. 4000   D. 5000

    12.____

13. 1 nanohenry would convert to _____ millihenries.

    A. .001   B. .0001   C. .00001   D. .0000001

    13.____

14. If 7 milliamps were converted to microamps, the answer would be _____ microamps.

    A. 7000   B. 700   C. 70   D. 7

    14.____

15. If two resistors are in parallel and are 100 ohms each, the total resistance is

    A. 100   B. 150   C. 50   D. 10

    15.____

16. In reference to the circuit in Question 15, if the first resistor has 25 volts DC, (VDC) across it, the second resistor also has 25 VDC across it, and there are no other components in the circuit except for the power source, the total circuit voltage is _____ VDC.

    A. 25   B. 50   C. 250   D. 500

    16.____

17. In reference to the circuit in Question 15, if the first resistor has 1 amp on it, and the second resistor also has 1 amp on it, the total circuit amperage is _____ amps.

    A. 1   B. 2   C. 3   D. 4

    17.____

18. If two resistors are in series and are 100 ohms each, the total resistance is

    A. 50   B. 100   C. 150   D. 200

    18.____

19. In reference to the circuit in Question 18, if the first resistor has 25 VDC across it and the second resistor also has 25 VDC across it, the total circuit voltage is

    A. 50   B. 100   C. 200   D. 500

    19.____

20. In reference to the circuit in Question 18, if the first resistor has 1 amp across it and the second resistor also has 1 amp on it, the total circuit amperage is

    A. 1   B. 5   C. 10   D. 15

    20.____

21. Where two resistors are in parallel, one is 100 ohms and the other is 300 ohms. The total resistance is _____ ohms.

    A. 25   B. 35   C. 55   D. 75

22. Three resistors in series are 25 ohms, 50 ohms, and 75 ohms, respectively. The total resistance is _____ ohms.

    A. 25   B. 50   C. 100   D. 150

23. Two inductors are in parallel; the first is 50 henries and the second is also 50 henries. The total inductance is _____ henries.

    A. 25   B. 50   C. 55   D. 60

24. Two inductors are in series and the first is 50 henries; the second is 50 henries. The total inductance is _____ henries.

    A. 25   B. 50   C. 75   D. 100

25. Where two inductors are in parallel, the first is 100 henries and the second is 200 henries. The total inductance is _____ henries.

    A. 50   B. 75   C. 65   D. 100

KEY (CORRECT ANSWERS)

1. C	6. D	11. B	16. A	21. D
2. A	7. A	12. D	17. B	22. D
3. B	8. B	13. D	18. D	23. A
4. A	9. D	14. A	19. A	24. D
5. B	10. A	15. C	20. A	25. B

TEST 2

DIRECTIONS: Each question or incomplete statement is followed by several suggested answers or completions. Select the one that BEST answers the question or completes the statement. *PRINT THE LETTER OF THE CORRECT ANSWER IN THE SPACE AT THE RIGHT.*

1. Two inductors are in series; the first inductor is 100 henries and the second is 200 henries.
   The total inductance is _____ henries.

   A. 200 B. 300 C. 400 D. 500

   1._____

2. Two capacitors are in parallel; each capacitor is 30 farads.
   The total capacitance is _____ farads.

   A. 60 B. 80 C. 100 D. 200

   2._____

3. Two capacitors are in series; each capacitor is 30 farads. The total capacitance is _____ farads.

   A. 10 B. 15 C. 20 D. 25

   3._____

4. Two capacitors are in parallel; the first is 50 farads and the second is 100 farads.
   The total capacitance is _____ farads.

   A. 50 B. 100 C. 125 D. 150

   4._____

5. Two capacitors are in series; the first is 50 farads and the second is 100 farads.
   The total capacitance is _____ farads.

   A. 33.333 B. 49.999 C. 13.333 D. 25.555

   5._____

6. A resistor's color codes are orange, blue, yellow, and gold, in that order.
   The value of the resistor is _____ kohms ± _____ %.

   A. 200; 2 B. 300; 4 C. 360; 5 D. 400; 7

   6._____

7. If a resistors color codes are red, black, and blue, the value of this resistor is _____ megohms ± _____ %.

   A. 20; 20 B. 40; 80 C. 30; 30 D. 50; 50

   7._____

8. If a resistor's color codes are gray, green, black, and silver, the resistor's value is _____ ohms ± _____ %.

   A. 55; 5 B. 75; 15 C. 85; 10 D. 100; 25

   8._____

9. One complete cycle of a sinewave takes 1000 microseconds. Its frequency is _____ hertz.

   A. 500 B. 1000 C. 2000 D. 5000

   9._____

10. If one complete cycle of a squarewave takes 5 microseconds, its frequency is _____ khertz.

    A. 200 B. 500 C. 700 D. 1000

    10._____

11. What is the PRT (pulse repetition time) of a 50 hertz (hz) sinewave? _____ milliseconds. 11._____

    A. 10   B. 20   C. 40   D. 60

12. The PRT of a 20 khz sawtooth signal is _____ megahertz. 12._____

    A. 50   B. 100   C. 200   D. 500

13. If a resistor measures 10 volts and 2 amps across it, the resistance is _____ ohms. 13._____

    A. 0   B. 2   C. 5   D. 10

14. If a 30 ohm resistor measures 10 volts, the power consumed by the resistor is _____ watts. 14._____

    A. 3000   B. 5000   C. 6500   D. 7000

15. If a 50 ohm resistor measures 4 amps across, the power consumed by it is _____ watts. 15._____

    A. 200   B. 400   C. 600   D. 800

16. If a 100 ohm resistor measures 25 volts across, the current on it is _____ amps. 16._____

    A. .15   B. .25   C. .55   D. .65

Questions 17-23.

DIRECTIONS: Questions 17 through 23 are to be answered on the basis of the following diagram.

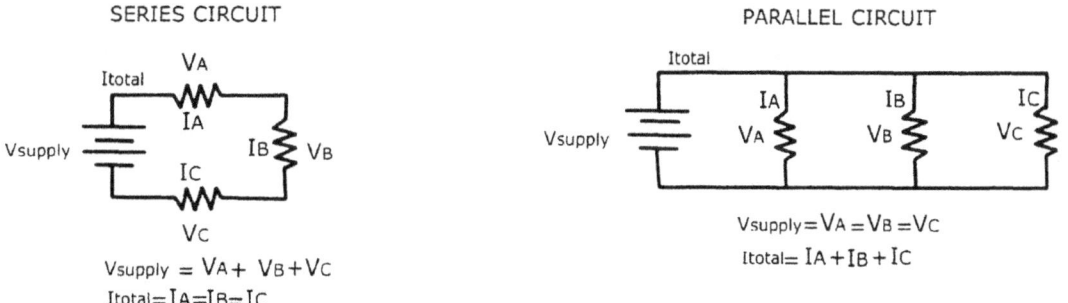

17. In the series circuit above, if Vsupply = 100 VDC, resistor A is 10 ohms, resistor B is 50 ohms, and resistor C is 5 ohms, the total circuit current is _____ amps. 17._____

    A. 1.538   B. 1.267   C. 1.358   D. 1.823

18. In the series circuit shown above, the current across each individual resistor is _____ amps. 18._____

    A. .5   B. 1.5   C. 2.5   D. 3.5

19. In the series circuit shown above, the total power drawn by the circuit is _____ watts.   19.____

    A. 140.25   B. 150.75   C. 153.38   D. 173.38

20. In the series circuit shown above, the power drawn from each individual resistor is   20.____
    _____ , _____ , and _____ watts, respectively.

    A. 23.65; 118.27; 11.827   B. 17.567; 123.27; 11.27
    C. 18.627; 145.27; 12.27   D. 21.735; 116.87; 11.83

21. In the parallel circuit shown above, if Vsupply = 100 VDC, resistor A is 10 ohms, resistor   21.____
    B is 50 ohms, and resistor C is 5 ohms, the total circuit current is _____ amps.

    A. 21   B. 27   C. 32   D. 45

22. In the parallel circuit shown above, the total power drawn by the circuit is _____ watts.   22.____

    A. 1200   B. 2300   C. 2700   D. 3200

23. In the parallel circuit above, the power drawn by each individual resistor is _____ watts,   23.____
    respectively.

    A. 100; 200; 2000   B. 200; 400; 5000
    C. 300; 500; 750   D. 450; 600; 1500

24. On an 0-scope display, one cycle of a signal takes up 4 1/2 divisions and the peak-to-   24.____
    peak amplitude of the signal takes up 3 3/4 divisions.
    With the volts/division knob set on 5 volts and the time/division knob set to 5 microsec-
    onds, the peak-to-peak amplitude and the frequency of the signal are _____ volts and
    _____ khz, respectively.

    A. 15.75; 100   B. 22.5; 200
    C. 37.5; 350   D. 45.75; 570

25. If a signal that has a peak-to-peak amplitude of 15 volts and a frequency of 5 megaherz   25.____
    is to be observed on an 0-scope with one complete cycle shown, the time/division knob
    and volts/division knob should be set on _____ microseconds and _____ volts per
    division, respectively.

    A. .02; 2   B. .05; 4   C. .07; 3.5   D. 10; 7.5

KEY (CORRECT ANSWERS)

1. B	6. C	11. B	16. B	21. C
2. A	7. A	12. A	17. A	22. D
3. B	8. C	13. C	18. B	23. A
4. D	9. B	14. A	19. C	24. B
5. A	10. A	15. D	20. A	25. A

ELECTRICITY
EXAMINATION SECTION
TEST 1

DIRECTIONS: Each question or incomplete statement is followed by several suggested answers or completions. Select the one that BEST answers the question or completes the statement. *PRINT THE LETTER OF THE CORRECT ANSWER IN THE SPACE AT THE RIGHT.*

1. The electrical code requires that the controller for an A.C. motor shall be capable of interrupting   1._____

    A. twice the full load current of the motor
    B. three times the full load current of the motor
    C. five times the full load current of the motor
    D. the stalled rotor current

2. The MINIMUM number of overload devices required for a 3Ø A.G. motor connected to a 120/208 volt system is   2._____

    A. 1   B. 2   C. 3   D. 4

3. A feeder tap shall be considered as properly protected when the smaller conductors terminate in a single properly sized set of fuses or a circuit breaker, provided the   3._____

    A. tap is not over 25 feet long
    B. tap is not over 15 feet long
    C. current carrying capacity of the tap is at least 1/3 the rating of the fuse or circuit breaker protecting the main
    D. tap is not over 25 feet long and its current carrying capacity is at least 1/3 the rating of the fuse protecting the main

4. Branch circuit conductors supplying a motor shall have a current carrying capacity, in percentage of the full load current rating of the motor, of NOT less than   4._____

    A. 100%   B. 125%   C. 150%   D. 200%

5. The motor disconnecting means shall be located   5._____
    A. within 10 feet of the motor   B. within sight of the controller
    B. within 15 feet of the motor   C. where convenient

6. The motor disconnecting means shall have a continuous duty rating, in percentage of the name plate current rating of the motor, of AT LEAST   6._____

    A. 100%   B. 115%   C. 150%   D. 125%

7. An externally operable switch may be used as a starter for a motor not over 2 HP and not over 300 volts provided it has a rating of AT LEAST_____of the _____ current of the motor.   7._____

    A. 200%; stalled rotor   B. 200%; full load
    C. 115%; full load   D. 150%; stalled rotor

67

8. A single disconnecting means may serve a group of motors provided   8._____

   A. all motors are 1/2 HP or less
   B. all motors are within a short distance from each other
   C. all motors are located within a single room and within sight of the disconnecting means
   D. one-half of the motors are located within a single room and within sight of the disconnecting means

9. A single-throw knife switch should be mounted so that   9._____

   A. gravity tends to close it
   B. it is in a vertical position
   C. it is accessible only to qualified persons
   D. gravity tends to open it

10. For oil burner motors, the disconnecting means shall be placed   10._____

    A. on the oil burner
    B. at the entrance to the basement
    C. inside the oil burner room
    D. not necessary

11. The MAIN reason for grounding conduit is to prevent it from becoming   11._____

    A. corroded by electrolysis
    B. magnetized
    C. accidentally energized at a higher potential than ground
    D. a source of radio interference

12. Large wires or cables are to pulled through conduit where there are a number of bends. This operation may be made easier by applying to the surface of these wires or cables a limited quantity of   12._____

    A. soapstone or talc   B. oil
    C. grease   D. rosin

13. Assume that a poly-phase synchronous converter having a field splitting or sectionalizing switch and a series field diverter is to be started from the A.C. side. When starting from the A.C. side, the sectionalizing switch should be _____ and the diverter should be _____.   13._____

    A. closed; closed   B. closed; opened
    C. opened; closed   D. opened; opened

14. In the electrical trade, the tool USUALLY used for bending small size pipe is a   14._____

    A. pipe hickey   B. grooved sheave bender
    C. roller bender   D. pipe wrench

15. For supplying both motor and lighting load, the type of A.C. distribution system commonly used is _____ wire.

    A. 2Ø - 4   B. 1Ø - 3   C. 3Ø - 3   D. 3Ø - 4

16. A set of conductors originating at a distribution center other than the main distribution center, and supplying one or more branch circuit distribution centers, is known as

    A. subservice   B. main   C. subfeeder   D. feeder

17. A lighting distribution panel board is to be fed from a 1Ø 3-wire grounded neutral A.C. feeder.
    The MAXIMUM number of 2-wire branch circuits that this panel board may supply is

    A. 20   B. 36   C. 42   D. any number

18. The type of socket that must be used for a 500 watt incandescent lamp is _____ base.

    A. screw shell medium   B. mogul
    C. intermediate   D. candelabra

19. The number of quarter bends between conduit fitting or boxes including those at the fitting or box shall NOT exceed

    A. 2   B. 4   C. 6   D. 8

20. A grounding conductor for portable or fixed equipment shall be
    A. white   B. grey   C. green   D. black

21. One foot of a certain size of nichrome wire has a resistance of 2 ohms.
    To make a heating element for a 600 watt, 120 volt toaster, the number of feet required is
    A. 5   B. 10   C. 12   D. 24

22. Which of the following wires has the LARGEST current carrying capacity?

    A. Asbestos   B. Rubber
    C. Waxed cotton   D. Thermoplastic

23. According to the electrical code, the sum of the continuous rating of the load consuming apparatus connected to the system or part of the system is defined as the _____ load of the system.

    A. computed   B. connected   C. calculated   D. rated

24. When fuses are used as motor protection, they shall be placed in

    A. all ungrounded conductors
    B. all conductors
    C. all but one ungrounded conductor
    D. half of the ungrounded conductors

25. Except for circuits of a system having a grounded neutral having no conductor at more than 150 volts to ground, plug fuses shall not be used in circuits where the voltage EXCEEDS _____ volts.   25._____

   A. 110 B. 125 C. 150 D. 250

KEY (CORRECT ANSWERS)

1. D
2. B
3. D
4. B
5. B

6. B
7. B
8. C
9. D
10. B

11. C
12. A
13. D
14. A
15. D

16. C
17. C
18. B
19. B
20. C

21. C
22. A
23. B
24. A
25. B

TEST 2

DIRECTIONS: Each question or incomplete statement is followed by several suggested answers or completions. Select the one that BEST answers the question or completes the statement. *PRINT THE LETTER OF THE CORRECT ANSWER IN THE SPACE AT THE RIGHT.*

1. Collector wires for a crane are supported at 25 foot intervals. The MINIMUM wire size that may be used is #

    A. 2   B. 4   C. 6   D. 8

2. It is necessary to space insulating supports for main collector wires of a crane forty feet apart.
The wires run on the same horizontal plane must be separated_____inches.

    A. 3   B. 6   C. 8   D. 12

3. A reverse phase relay is a device which is PRIMARILY used

    A. to reverse rotation of 3-phase induction motors
    B. to prevent accidental reversal of a polyphase motor
    C. to reverse the current in case one phase is reversed
    D. as an overload relay for 3-phase motors

4. A 3Ø motor used on a crane or a hoist

    A. will not start if one phase is not live
    B. will not start with all resistance inserted
    C. will not start if brake solenoid is energized
    D. may use a common return wire

5. A branch circuit feed for a crane motor that runs through a room where the temperature exceeds 167° F (75° C) shall be type

    A. R
    B. SB
    C. AF
    D. fire retarded

6. A common return is used to feed 2 – 3Ø crane motors. It shall be

    A. installed in rigid conduit
    B. type AVA
    C. not permitted
    D. individually bushed

7. Surgical operating rooms GENERALLY shall be considered_____hazardous location(s).

    A. Class I   B. Class II   C. Class III   D. not a

8. Electrical installations in garages, unless located at least four feet above the floor, shall be governed by the requirements for

    A. Class I
    B. Class II
    C. Class III
    D. General wiring

9. Portable extension light cords used in a garage shall NOT exceed _____ feet.

   A. 8   B. 15   C. 20   D. 40

10. An underground service to a private garage shall be
    A. lead-covered conductors in rigid conduit or other approved types buried 18" or more
    B. lead-covered conductors in rigid conduit buried 12"
    C. lead-covered conductors in E.M.T. buried 18"
    D. type R conductors in rigid conduit buried 18"

11. High tension conductors for a skeleton sign shall

    A. be insulated for 10,000 volts
    B. be insulated for 15,000 volts
    C. be insulated for 30,000 volts
    D. not be used

12. Emergency lighting in a theatre shall be controlled

    A. from the stage lighting control
    B. from the lobby
    C. by double pole switches
    D. from the operators booth

13. The MINIMUM size system grounding conductor shall be NOT less than #

    A. 16   B. 8   C. 4   D. 1/0

14. If you had a choice of connecting to one of the following grounding electrodes, you would use

    A. buried plates
    B. driven rod
    C. gas piping system
    D. continuous metallic underground active water piping system

15. Grounding electrodes other than water piping systems shall have a resistance to ground NOT exceeding _____ ohms.

    A. 0   B. 5   C. 25   D. infinity

16. A grounding conductor for portable or fixed equipment shall be

    A. white   B. grey   C. green   D. black

17. The MAXIMUM number of outlets allowed on a 20 ampere branch lighting circuit is

    A. 2   B. 8   C. 10   D. 20

18. The MAXIMUM number of mogul sockets that may be used on a 115 volt heavy duty lampholder branch circuit is

    A. 2   B. 8   C. 10   D. 20

19. The voltage drop in a 120 volt lighting circuit should be kept to a minimum and may NOT Exceed _____ volts.

    A. 120　　　B. 5.2　　　C. 3　　　D. 2.5

20. A wire 100 feet long is divided into two parts so that the ratio of their lengths is 4/1. The length of the longer piece is _____ feet.

    A. 10　　　B. 20　　　C. 40　　　D. 80

21. An effect caused by dissimilar metals is known as

    A. thermoelectric　　　B. thermopile
    C. thermostatic　　　D. thermionic

22. With the weight of water used as a base, the ratio of weight to other liquids is known as
    A. density　　　B. specific gravity
    C. viscosity　　　D. buoyancy

23. A utility company would supply a lighting and power load with _____ wire service.

    A. 1∅ -3　　　B. 2∅ -3　　　C. 3∅ -3　　　D. 3∅ -4

24. A ballast in a fluorescent fixture is used to

    A. reduce A.C. hum　　　B. limit the current
    C. lower capacitor voltage　　　D. eliminate cycle flicker

25. A fluorescent lamp being basically an A.C. lamp

    A. cannot be used D.C.
    B. may be made adaptable for D.C. by connecting a fixed resistor of the proper value in series with the line and auxiliary
    C. may be used for D.C. providing the operating voltage is the same as that required for A.C.
    D. can be used on D.C. only when available voltage is higher than that required for operation on A.C.

KEY (CORRECT ANSWERS)

1.	C	11.	B
2.	D	12.	B
3.	B	13.	B
4.	A	14.	D
5.	B	15.	C
6.	C	16.	C
7.	A	17.	D
8.	A	18.	C
9.	D	19.	B
10.	A	20.	D

21.	A
22.	B
23.	D
24.	B
25.	B

TEST 3

DIRECTIONS: Each question or incomplete statement is followed by several suggested answers or completions. Select the one that BEST answers the question or completes the statement. *PRINT THE LETTER OF THE CORRECT ANSWER IN THE SPACE AT THE RIGHT.*

1. The MAXIMUM voltage to ground for elevator control pushbuttons is _____ volts.

    A. 120   B. 208   C. 300   D. 600

2. The MINIMUM size equipment grounding conductor for high tension vertical distribution transformer cases is #

    A. 10   B. 8   C. 000   D. 0000

3. Vertical conduits for high tension steel armored cable shall be supported by building construction at intervals NOT exceeding _____ feet and encased in _____ inches of concrete.

    A. 25; 2   B. 35; 2   C. 35; 3   D. 25; 3

4. The MINIMUM distance that shall be maintained between bare metal parts having a potential difference of 125 volts on panelboards is

    A. 3/4"   B. 1"   C. 1 1/4"   D. 1 1/2"

5. The frequency of the current at a load, as compared to that of the generator,

    A. depends on the load
    B. is lower
    C. is higher
    D. is the same

6. The resistance to the flow of magnetic flux is known as

    A. permeance
    B. reluctance
    C. resistance
    D. reactance

7. A conductor cutting magnetic lines of force at the rate of 10^8 lines per second will generate 1

    A. ohm   B. ampere   C. watt   D. volt

8. An inverse time delay relay will operate _____ current.

    A. slower, the greater the
    B. faster, the greater the
    C. faster, the smaller the
    D. at the same speed regardless of the amount of

9. A 120 volt system feeds an arc lamp that is to operate at 15 amps, at 62 volts. What resistance must be inserted in the line for PROPER operation? _____ ohms.

    A. .26   B. 3.86   C. 4.13   D. 8

10. If you reversed the line leads to a D.C. compound motor, it would

    A. stop
    B. reverse
    C. run in the same direction
    D. slow down

11. A D.C. generator has an EMF of 115 volts and an internal resistance of .07 ohms. What is the voltage at the load when it is delivering 50 amperes?

    A. 111.5 B. 115 C. 118.5 D. 120

12. The sockets allowed for a 500 watt incandescent lamp is

    A. candelabra
    B. intermediate
    C. medium
    D. mogul

13. A single circuit may be used to feed several small motors, providing the largest motor does NOT exceed _____ amps.

    A. 6 B. 10 C. 15 D. 20

14. A compensator is a device used with induction motors to

    A. compensate for electrical losses of the motor
    B. compensate for volt drop in the motor
    C. increase the starting torque of the motor
    D. decrease the line voltage at starting

15. A 2 HP 3-phase 220 volt squirrel cage motor would USUALLY be started by means of a(n)

    A. compensator
    B. 3 or 4 point starting box
    C. reduced voltage starter
    D. across the line starter

16. The type of starting and speed control equipment that would be used for a 50 HP wound rotor induction motor is

    A. with resistors connected in rotor circuit
    B. a 3 point starting box
    C. an autotransformer (compensator)
    D. an automatic primary resistor type of starter

17. In order to reverse rotation of a 3-phase squirrel cage induction motor, you would reverse

    A. any two line leads
    B. all line leads
    C. the brush leads
    D. starting winding leads

18. Reversing direction of rotation of a 3Ø wound rotor motor could be done by reversing _____ leads.

    A. all slip-ring B. all line C. two slip-ring D. two line

19. To change direction of rotation of a 4-wire 2-phase motor,

    A. interchange the leads of one phase
    B. interchange the leads of both phases
    C. reverse the leads from the slip rings
    D. do nothing, it cannot be readily reversed

20. In selecting a reversing type motor starter, for maximum protection, you would choose one that is

    A. separately controlled
    B. mechanically and electrically interlocked
    C. electrically interlocked
    D. mechanically interlocked

21. A 3∅ wound rotor motor running at full speed suddenly drops to half speed. The PROBABLE cause is

    A. the stator field is shorted
    B. a rotor winding shorted due to centrifugal force
    C. a rotor lead disconnected due to centrifugal force
    D. two rotor leads rubbing against each other

22. Of the following types of motors, the one that requires both A.C. and D.C. for operation is the ____ motor.

    A. universal   B. compound
    C. squirrel cage   D. synchronous

23. If the D.C. field of a synchronous motor is overexcited,

    A. it will run faster
    B. it will run slower
    C. line current will be leading
    D. it will hunt

24. A starter used for a synchronous motor would be

    A. an autotransformer   B. a resistor
    C. a rotor starter   D. the star-delta type

25. A 3∅ squirrel cage motor has 12 leads because

    A. it is a 6-phase motor
    B. they are stator and rotor leads
    C. 2 parallel leads are used on each winding
    D. the windings are used in parallel or series

KEY (CORRECT ANSWERS)

1. C
2. D
3. A
4. A
5. D

6. B
7. D
8. B
9. B
10. C

11. A
12. D
13. A
14. D
15. D

16. A
17. A
18. D
19. A
20. B

21. C
22. D
23. C
24. A
25. D

TEST 4

DIRECTIONS: Each question or incomplete statement is followed by several suggested answers or completions. Select the one that BEST answers the question or completes the statement. *PRINT THE LETTER OF THE CORRECT ANSWER IN THE SPACE AT THE RIGHT.*

1. To reverse direction of rotation of a split-phase motor, you would   1.____

    A. do nothing as it cannot be done
    B. reverse the line leads
    C. reverse polarity of all windings
    D. reverse polarity of starting winding

2. To reverse a capacitor motor, you would reverse   2.____

    A. both auxiliary and main windings
    B. the line leads
    C. the condenser
    D. the auxiliary winding

3. In a capacitor motor, the condenser is connected   3.____

    A. in series with the field
    B. across the motor terminals
    C. in parallel with the starting winding
    D. in series with the starting winding

4. To reverse the direction of a repulsion-induction motor, you should   4.____

    A. move the brushes so they cross the pole axis
    B. interchange terminal connections
    C. reverse the starting winding
    D. change the connections to the armature

5. To reverse rotation of a shaded pole motor, you would   5.____

    A. reverse the armature leads
    B. reverse the field leads
    C. shift the brushes
    D. do nothing as the motor cannot be readily reversed

6. A split-phase motor runs hot at no load.   6.____
   The probable reason is the
    A. starting winding is open
    B. starting winding is reversed
    C. centrifugal switch is broken
    D. running winding is completely shorted

7. The difference between the operating speed and the synchronous speed of an induction machine is called the

   A. slip B. phase C. acceleration D. frequency

8. The speed, in R.P.M., of a 10-pole, 60 cycle, 3∅ alternator is MOST NEARLY

   A. 3600 B. 4800 C. 1440 D. 720

9. A 2300 volt 80% PF, 60 cycle, 8-pole synchronous motor may be DIRECTLY connected to a pump designed for a speed of _____ RPM.

   A. 600 B. 900 C. 1200 D. 1800

10. The rated speed of a three-phase, 4-pole squirrel cage, 60 cycle motor is MOST NEARLY _____ RPM.

    A. 900 B. 1200 C. 1750 D. 1800

11. The synchronous speed of a 4-pole, 25 cycle motor is

    A. 750 RPM B. 375 RPM C. 3750 RPM D. not fixed

12. Three and four way switches are connected

    A. in series with the line
    B. across the line
    C. to the neutral
    D. only loads less than 5 amps

13. Travelers are distinguished by being

    A. not connected to a current consuming device
    B. connected to one hot line
    C. connected to a current consuming device
    D. connected to a grounded line

14. Of the following types of single phase induction motors, the one that produces the HIGHEST starting torque is by the _____ method.

    A. shaded pole
    B. repulsion start
    C. resistance split phase
    D. capacitor split phase

15. The break down torque will vary on a squirrel cage induction motor with a given slip _____ the voltage.

    A. inversely with
    B. with the square of
    C. with the
    D. with the square root of

16. A 95% efficient transformer supplies a 114 KW load. The input is _____ KW.

    A. 5.7 B. 108 C. 114 D. 120

17. A D.C. motor that takes 40 amperes at 250 volts delivers 10 horsepower. The efficiency of this motor is APPROXIMATELY

    A. 55%   B. 64%   C. 75%   D. 100%

18. A 5 HP 220 volt D.C. motor that has an efficiency of 90% takes a full load current of APPROXIMATELY _____ amps.

    A. 143   B. 17   C. 18.8   D. 20.5

19. A 20 HP D.C. motor is 85% efficient. The power, in kilowatts, that it will take from the line is

    A. 12.7   B. 17.5   C. 20.0   D. 23.5

20. The current taken by a 1 HP 120 volt single-phase induction motor whose efficiency is 90% and power factor of 0.8 is _____ amps.

    A. 6.9   B. 7.8   C. 8.6   D. 6.2

21. If electricity costs 3¢ per KWH, what is the cost of running a 440 volt 3Ø 10 HP motor whose efficiency is 80% for one hour?

    A. 3¢   B. 18¢   C. 22¢   D. 28¢

22. Three motor control start-stop pushbutton stations are connected
    A. in series
    B. in parallel
    C. three way
    D. in series-parallel

23. The torque of a D.C. shunt motor varies as the _____
    A. armature current
    B. cube of armature current
    C. field current squared
    D. square of the armature current

24. For fast stopping, a braking method sometimes utilizes a motor as a generator to create a retarding force.
This method is known as

    A. magnetic braking
    B. dynamic braking
    C. counter EMF braking
    D. plugging

25. An instrument used to measure the angular speed of a motor is the
    A. tachometer
    B. micrometer
    C. monometer
    D. speedometer

KEY (CORRECT ANSWERS)

1.	D	11.	A
2.	D	12.	A
3.	D	13.	A
4.	A	14.	A
5.	D	15.	B
6.	C	16.	D
7.	A	17.	C
8.	D	18.	C
9.	B	19.	B
10.	C	20.	C

21. D
22. D
23. A
24. B
25. A

TEST 5

DIRECTIONS: Each question or incomplete statement is followed by several suggested answers or completions. Select the one that BEST answers the question or completes the statement. *PRINT THE LETTER OF THE CORRECT ANSWER IN THE SPACE AT THE RIGHT.*

1. Interpoles are
    A. connected in series with the shunt field
    B. connected in parallel with the armature
    C. used to increase the degree of compounding
    D. used to improve commutation

1._____

2. In the D.C. shunt motor, the field
    A. has comparatively few turns of wire
    B. has comparatively many turns of wire
    C. is connected in series with the armature
    D. current is more than the line current

2._____

3. If, in a compound motor, the series and shunt fields oppose each other, the motor
    A. is differential compound
    B. is cumulative compound
    C. will not run
    D. will overheat

3._____

4. A cumulative compound motor has _____ set(s) of fields.
    A. 1   B. 2   C. 3   D. 4

4._____

5. To reverse rotation of a D.C. shunt motor, you would
    A. reverse the line leads
    B. reverse the series fields
    C. reverse the armature connections
    D. shift the brushes

5._____

6. The PROPER way to reverse the direction of rotation of a compound motor is to interchange the
    A. line leads   B. armature connections
    C. shunt field connections   D. series field connections

6._____

7. If you attempted to start a D.C. compound motor in which the series field was open-circuited, the motor would
    A. not start   B. blow the fuse
    C. run away   D. start to reverse

7._____

8. If the field current of a shunt motor is decreased, the motor will
    A. run away   B. run slower
    C. run faster   D. overheat

8._____

9. To decrease the speed of a D.C. shunt wound motor below its name plate rating, it is advisable to connect

    A. resistance in the field circuit
    B. a shunt across the field circuit
    C. resistance in the armature circuit
    D. a shunt across the armature circuit

9._____

10. The reason for using a starting box for a D.C. motor is to

    A. reduce armature current during starting period
    B. increase the starting torque
    C. regulate the speed
    D. reduce voltage on fields during starting

10._____

11. The holding coil of a 3-point starting box is connected

    A. in series with the field
    B. in series with the line
    C. in series with the armature
    D. across the line

11._____

12. When replacing a D.C. blowout coil, it is MOST important to

    A. have its resistance the same as the old coil
    B. have its resistance higher than the old coil
    C. see that the magnetic field reacts
    D. install it when the contacts are open

12._____

13. The usual cause of localized heating of an armature is

    A. overload
    B. eddy currents
    C. armature out of center between poles
    D. shorted armature coil

13._____

14. What would happen when a D.C. motor is running with an open armature coil?

    A. Speed would increase.
    B. Speed would decrease.
    C. Motor would begin to spark violently.
    D. The coil would begin heating.

14._____

15. An electrical contractor files an application for inspection for a job
    A. when completed   B. when starting
    C. when half finished   D. before starting

15._____

16. Polarizing a fixture means

    A. attaching the fixture to the outlet box
    B. connecting identified conductor to shell of lampholder
    C. removing the insulation from the fixture wires
    D. connecting unidentified conductor to shell of lamp-holder

16._____

17. A closed circuit burglar alarm system is better than an open circuit system because   17._____

    A. it costs less to install
    B. it gives greater protection
    C. the bell will not ring if the wire is cut
    D. it requires fewer parts

18. A portable electric drill should be grounded by means of   18._____

    A. standard attachment plug
    B. 3-prong attachment plug
    C. T slot attachment plug
    D. cord connector

19. A single pole switch is ALWAYS connected in the   19._____

    A. neutral leg   B. white wire
    C. identified wire   D. live leg

20. The SAFEST way for an electrician to determine whether a circuit is A.C. or D.C. is to   20._____

    A. use a neon test lamp
    B. test bare parts with his fingertips
    C. telephone the Edison Company
    D. use an incandescent test lamp

21. Which of the following is NOT permitted for permanent wiring in New York City?   21._____

    A. Armored cable (BX)   B. Rigid conduit
    C. Romex   D. EMT

22. In rigid conduit work, the GREATEST number of quarter bends (90°) permitted between outlets is   22._____

    A. two   B. four   C. six   D. eight

23. The standard network system used for light and power in New York City is   23._____

    A. 110/220 volt single phase
    B. 220 volt 2 phase 3 wire
    C. 208/120 volt 3 phase 4 wire
    D. 120/240 volt single phase 3 wire

24. The SMALLEST size service entrance conductor permitted is   24._____

    A. #2   B. #4   C. #6   D. #8

25. The ampere rating of service switches must be AT LEAST _____ amperes.   25._____

    A. 60   B. 30   C. 200   D. 100

KEY (CORRECT ANSWERS)

1.	D	11.	A
2.	B	12.	D
3.	A	13.	D
4.	B	14.	C
5.	C	15.	D
6.	B	16.	B
7.	A	17.	B
8.	C	18.	B
9.	C	19.	C
10.	A	20.	A

21. C
22. B
23. C
24. A
25. D

ELECTRO-MECHANICAL NOTES AND RESOURCES

TABLE OF CONTENTS

		Page
I.	**BASIC ELECTRICITY**	1
	Ohm's Law	2
	Kirchoff's Voltage Law	3
	Kirchoff's Current Law	3
	Inductors	3
	Capacitors	4
	AC Cycles	4
	Magnetism	5
	Relays	6
	Switches	6
	Diodes	6
	Transistors	7
	Soldering	8
II.	**COMPUTERS**	8
	Numbering Systems	9
	Flip Flops	10
	Logic Gates	12
III.	**OSCILLOSCOPES**	12
	Meters	13
IV.	**SCIENTIFIC NOTATION**	14
V.	**GEARS**	14
	Pulleys	16
	Lubricants	18

ELECTRO-MECHANICAL NOTES AND RESOURCES
I. BASIC ELECTRICITY

Resistance is measured in ohms, and its symbol is Ω. Resistance is additive in series circuits. This means that with two resistors in series as shown below, if one resistor is 100Ω's and the other 200Ω's, then the total resistance is 300Ω's.

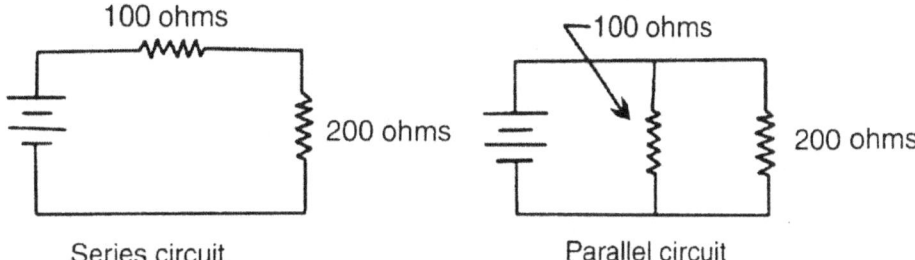

Series circuit   Parallel circuit

Resistance in parallel is summed differently. In the figure shown above in the parallel circuit, if the 100 ohm resistor is considered to be R, and the 200 ohm resistor is R, the formula is:

$$\frac{1}{R_t} = \frac{1}{R_1} + \frac{1}{R_2}.$$

Derivation is as follows:

$$\frac{1}{R_t} = (\frac{1}{R_1} \times \frac{R_2}{R_2}) + (\frac{1}{R_2} \times \frac{R_1}{R_1}) = \frac{R_1}{R_1 R_2} + \frac{R_1}{R_1 R_2} = \frac{R_1 + R_2}{R_1 R_2}$$

So, now we have:

$$\frac{1}{R_t} = \frac{R_1 + R_2}{R_1 R_2}. \text{ Inversing, } \frac{R_t}{1} = \frac{R_1 R_2}{R_1 + R_2} = R_t$$

This derivation is for two resistors in parallel; for more resistors in parallel, the same derivation technique would be followed.

Given that all the resistors in a parallel circuit are of the same resistive value, the following is a short calculation of the total circuit resistance.

Take the resistive value of one of the resistors and divide it by the number of resistors in the parallel circuit. Assuming that 5 resistors are in parallel and each one is 500 ohms, to calculate the total circuit resistance, divide 500 by 5 and the result is 100 ohms.

An interesting aspect of resistance is that the inverse (1/R) is conduction, the ease with which electrons can flow through a given material, and is expressed in units of *mhos* with a symbol that is the same as the resistance symbol inverted.

The color codes for resistors are as follows:

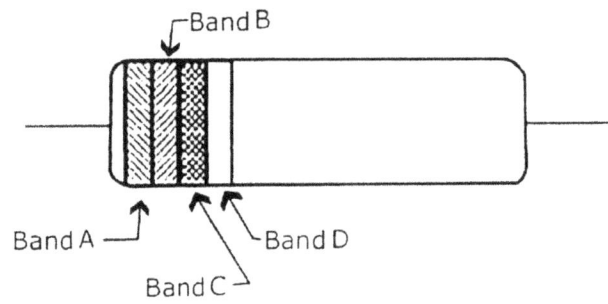

Band A is the first digit of the value of the resistor.
Band B is the second digit of the value of the resistor.
Band C is the decimal multiplier.
Band D is the tolerance of the value of the resistor.

The colors and their values are:

COLOR	VALUE	COLOR	VALUE	TOLERANCE COLORS
BLACK	0	GREEN	5	
BROWN	1	BLUE	6	GOLD 5%
RED	2	VIOLET	7	SILVER 10%
ORANGE	3	GRAY	8	NO COLOR 20%
YELLOW	4	WHITE	9	

So, a resistor colored as:
  1st band   violet
  2nd band   green
  3rd band   blue
  4th band   silver
is computed as:

75×10^6 ohms $\pm$ 10% or 75 megohms $\pm$ 10%

An easy way of remembering the sequence of the color codes above is to remember the following sentence and use the first letters of each word: *Bad Boys Race Our Young Girls Behind Victory Garden Walls*.

Ohms' Law

Ohm's law is the law that establishes the mathematical relationship of current, voltage, and resistance in a circuit. The formula is: $E = IR$, where E = the circuit or component voltage, I = the circuit or component current, and R = the circuit or component resistance.

In the circuit shown below, we know E = 10 volts and I=5 ohms. Deriving the formula, we get $I = E/R$. So, I = 10/5 = 2 amps.

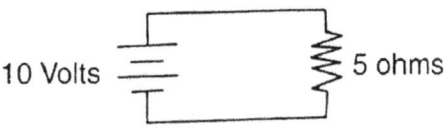

The power consumed by a component is equal to E x I. So, P = EI, and this calculated value is expressed in units of watts.

Kirchoff's Voltage Law

Kirchoff's voltage law states in technical terms that in a simple series circuit, as shown below, the algebraic sum of the voltages around the circuit is zero. Basically, this means that the supply voltage, Vsupply, is equal to VA + VB + VC, which are the voltage drops across the respective resistors in the circuit below. In the parallel circuit shown below, the voltages in each of the individual branches are equal to each other as well as equal to the total circuit voltage.

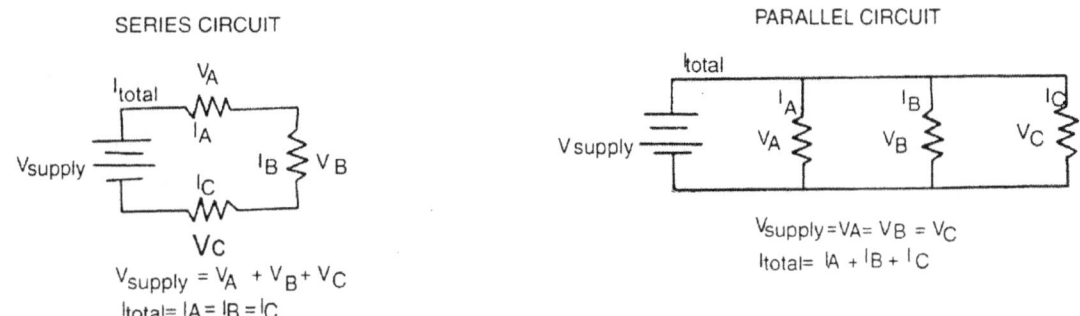

Kirchoff's Current Law

Kirchoff's current law states that at any junction of conductors in a circuit, the algebraic sum of the currents is zero. On a series circuit shown above, current is equal across each individual component as well as equal to the total circuit current. In a parallel circuit, the current across each individual branch when added is equal to the total circuit current, as in the parallel circuit shown above.

Inductors

Inductors are coils that oppose changes in current, which also store energy in a magnetic field. Induction is expressed in units of henries, and represented by an h. Inductance in series and parallel circuits is summed in the same manner as resistance. Inductors tend to block AC signals and pass DC voltages. An inductor's ability to oppose AC current is called inductive reactance. Inductive reactance is expressed in ohms just like resistance, but is represented by the symbol ZL, where Z means impedance and L added specifies inductive reactance or impedance. The impedance symbol Ω should not be confused with the resistive symbol, which is the same. The formula for inductive reactance is: $X_L = 2\pi fL$, where $\pi = 3.14$, f = the frequency of the AC signal to be used, and L = the inductance in henries. The schematic symbol for an inductor is

Adding two lines on the top of the symbol means that it is an iron core filled inductor. Since they have a magnetic field, they are used in transformers and electromagnetic switches.

Capacitors

Capacitors consist basically of two metal plates in parallel separated by an insulator (dielectric). Capacitors have the ability to store a charge in an electrostatic field between its two plates. This charge is dependent upon two things, the capacitance of the circuit and the difference in the potential of the circuit. The capacitance of a capacitor is measured in farads, and is depicted by the letter C. Capacitance is summed in a manner that is exactly opposite to that of resistors, since it is directly summed when in parallel as shown below.

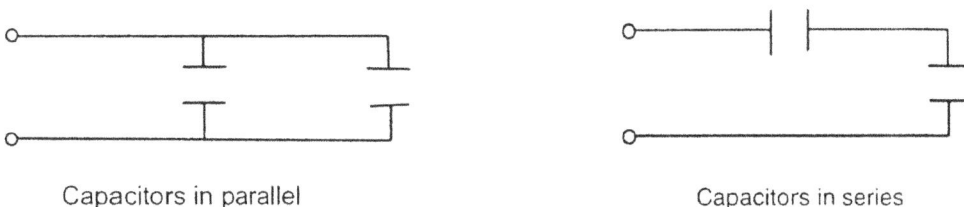

Capacitors in parallel   Capacitors in series

In the parallel circuit shown above, if one of the capacitors is 1 farad and the other is 2 farads, then total circuit capacitance is 3 farads. Capacitance of such a high value is rare and usually limited to industrial use. More realistic values would be in the microfarad range. When capacitors are in series as shown above, they are added, as are resistors in parallel. So, the formula would be: $C_t = \dfrac{C_1 C_2}{C_1 + C_2}$

As with inductors, capacitors are also measured by the opposition that they may give to AC current flow, which is called capacitive reactance. Capacitive reactance, X_c, is expressed also in units of ohms, and its formula is:

$$X_c = \dfrac{1}{2\Pi f C}$$

where f = the frequency in hertz of the AC signal, and C = the capacitance, in farads. Electrolytic capacitors are polarized, which means that they must be placed in circuits with polarity considerations.

AC Cycles

The five main forms of AC signals are sawtooth, sinusoidal, square, rectangular, and trapezoidal waveforms.

Sawtooth waveform   Sinusoidal waveform   Square waveform   Rectangular waveform   Trapazoidal waveform

There are also parts of sinewaves that are of interest.

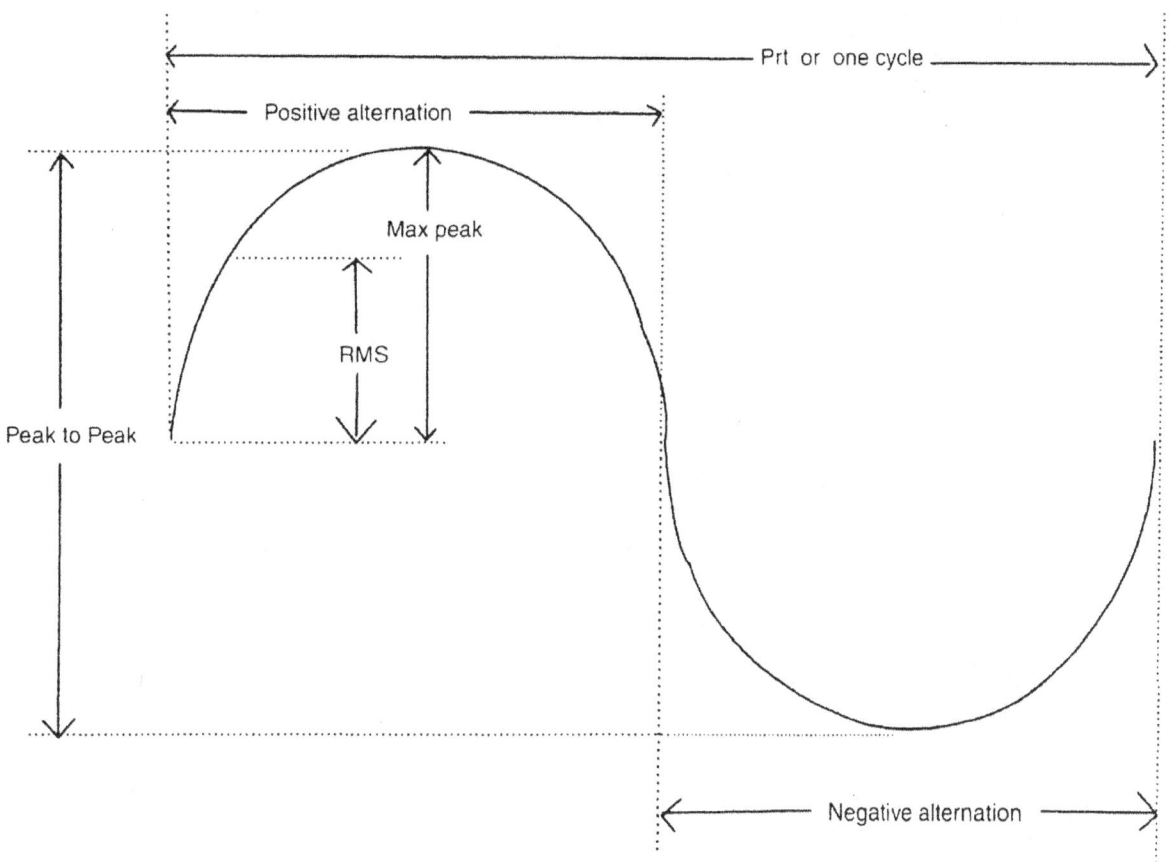

The RMS value (root mean square) is the same as the effective value, which is the value of an AC signal that has the same power or heating effect as a DC voltage. With sinusoidal waveforms, this value is equal to .707 times the AC voltage peak.

The average value is the value of an AC signal of a positive alternation and in a sinusoidal waveform is equal to .637 times the maximum voltage or peak.

Magnetism

The basic properties of magnetism are permeability, reluctance, and retentivity.

Permeability is the property of the ease with which a metal will allow magnetic lines of flux to pass through it.

Reluctance is a property of a metal that opposes lines of flux going through it.

Retentivity is the ability of a magnetized metal to stay magnetized.

Permanent magnets have high retentivity. Steel has high retentivity, low permeability, and high reluctance. Soft iron has low retentivity, high permeability, and low reluctance.

When a wire has current passing through it, the wire will have an electromagnetic field around it. The left hand rule can be used to determine the direction of the electromagnetic lines. To do this, place your left hand with fingers wrapped around the wire and your thumb pointed in the direction of current flow. The direction in which your fingers are pointing is the direction of the electromagnetic lines of flux.

Relays

The three types of relays are power relays, control relays, and sensing relays. Power relays control high voltages going to circuits such as motors. Control relays are used to energize and de-energize other relays and associated circuitry. Sensing relays are used to detect such items as over or under, current or voltages. When sensed by the sensing relay, power sources will be disconnected.

Switches

The various types of switches are identified by the number of poles, throws, and positions that they have. The number of *poles* that a switch has indicates the number of terminals through which voltages may enter the switch. The number of *throws* refers to the number of circuits that could be completed or disconnected by each blade or contacter. The number of *positions* indicates the number of different places that the toggle of the switch can be placed in.
The four kinds of switches are shown below.

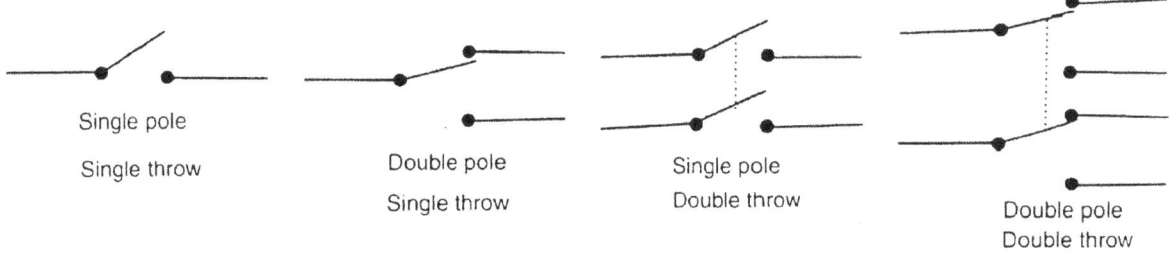

Single pole
Single throw

Double pole
Single throw

Single pole
Double throw

Double pole
Double throw

Diodes

As its name implies, a simple rectifier diode is used for signal rectification. The schematic symbol is shown below. Zener diodes are designed for specific reverse breakdown voltages; and since they keep the voltage across the diode constant, they are used for voltage regulation. Tunnel diodes will give negative resistance for specific ranges of forward bias voltages. Because of this phenomenon, tunnel diodes are used as amplifiers or oscillators. Silicon controlled rectifiers (SCR) are triggered diodes. These are used to control AC voltages on one particular half cycle. Diacs work on both sides of the cycles of an AC signal. Triacs are gated diacs. Basically, SCRs, diacs, and triacs are used to pick out desired portions of AC signals.

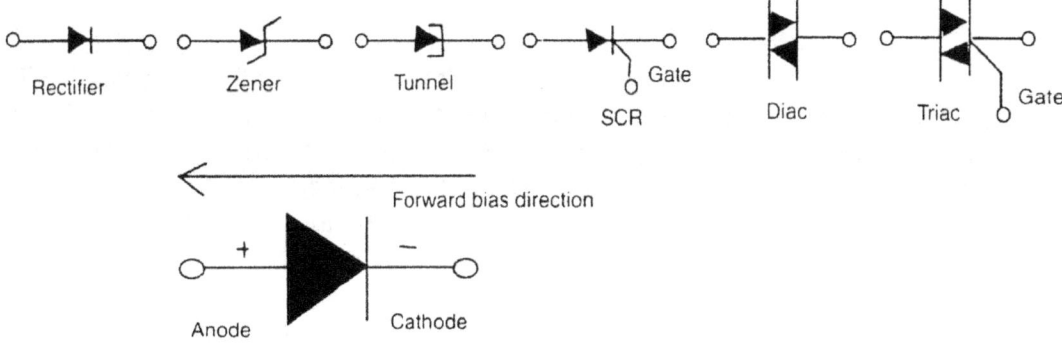

Transistors

Transistors are solid state devices that can act as amplifiers or switches. They are classified as bipolar and field-effect transistors. The bipolar transistor allows current flow in either direction. The two types of bipolar transistors are PNP and NPN transistors, which are shown below.

PNP transistor

NPN transistor

When used strictly as a switch, the PNP transistor requires a negative input signal on the base to turn it on or conduct. Conversely, the NPN transistor requires a positive signal on the base to turn it on.

Bipolar transistors are not only used as switches and have several configurations. The different transistor configurations and their respective traits are shown below:

BEG
VPI
ABG
LMH
HML
IOI

The first line is the type of configuration, i.e., common base, emitter, or collector. The particular transistor's configuration traits are shown vertically below the transistor. Line two shows electrical gains (voltage, power, or current). Line three shows the type of gain (alpha, beta, or gamma). Line four shows the input impedance of the configuration (low, medium, or high). Line five shows the output impedance (high, medium, or low).

Line <u>six</u> shows the output signal phase relationship with the input (in-phase or out-of-phase).

There are two types of field effect transistors (FET) - JFETs and MOSFETs. <u>JFETs</u> stand for junction field transistors and control large voltages with very small inputs and, therefore, can be used as amplifiers. <u>MOSFETs</u> stands for metal-oxide-semiconductor field effect transistors and have a higher input impedance and can use even smaller signals. They are also smaller and are configured by the thousands to form chips.

Soldering

Electrical connections are joined by soldering. Soldering requires a high heat source and an alloy that melts at a relatively low temperature when compared to other metals. The basic soldering technique is to first heat the joint to be soldered with a soldering device and then place the solder directly onto the joint with the soldering device still in contact. Allow the solder to melt and flow onto the joint surface covering the joint area. Once this occurs, remove solder and device, allowing to cool without any movement of the joint area. After the solder hardens, inspect the solder joint. The joint should look smooth, bright, and shiny, with the surface area of the joint smoothly covered. If the solder has the appearance of being partially balled up instead of a smooth semi-flat flow, it is called a *cold solder* joint. A possible cause of a cold solder joint might be wrongly applying the solder to the solder device and then dropping onto the area to be soldered. If the solder joint is not shiny but dull and gray instead, then the connection was probably moved prior to the solder hardening completely.

Solder is an alloy usually made up of various ratios and combinations of tin and lead. Some that are resin filled are also called flux. Soldering fluxes are used to de-oxide surfaces that are being soldered. One type of flux is acid-core resin, which is very corrosive to electrical connections and should be avoided.

Soldering devices come in various sizes, depending on the job required to be done. One of the most delicate of soldering jobs, soldering components with very small connections onto printed circuit boards, is usually done by pencil irons. These miniature irons are ideal for providing low heat to small areas. Soldering jobs that require more heat use items such as solder guns. These produce high heat and heat up very quickly.

The types of solder tips most commonly used in electrical work are made of copper or copper alloys, since copper has high heat conductivity and good tinning quality. The tinning of a soldering tip increases heat transfer/conductivity to the area to be soldered and also reduces scaling of the solder tip. Tinning consists of getting a good layer of solder on the working surface of the copper tip. Cleaning tips that become dirty or discolored requires dipping the tip in water while hot, and quickly removing it or wiping with a damp sponge or towel.

II. COMPUTERS

The 5 major components of a computer are input, storage, control unit, arithmetic and "logic unit, and output. The <u>input</u> device allows information such as data and commands or instructions to be fed into the computer system. The most common type of input device is the keyboard. Other input devices are magnetic and optical readers. <u>Storage</u> devices are used to store memory, such as instructions or data until they are needed. Memory is stored in bits, which is the most basic element of binary numbers, a 1 or 0. Bytes are groups of eight bits. A nibble is half of a byte. The <u>control unit</u> coordinates the operations of the entire computer. It interprets programs and issues instructions to accomplish the program. The <u>output</u> device communicates the progress or results of a program used in the computer to the operator/user. The devices range from monitor screens to high speed printers.

Numbering Systems

Computers and associated circuitry use several numbering systems that have different bases. We are all familiar with base 10 numbering system. This is the system we use in everyday life. In this system, each decimal/digit place represents a value of 10, whether it is the first digit to the left of the decimal point, which is a 10 to the 0 power or one's. The second digit to the left represents the number of 10's and the third represents the number of 100's.

The other base sytems work in the same fashion with their own respective bases. The other base systems used are base 2 (binary), base 8 (octal), and base 16 (hexadecimal). It is easy to convert from one system to another.

	5th digit	4th digit	3rd digit	2nd digit	1st digit
Base 10	10^4	10^3	10^2	10^1	10^0
Base 2	2^4	2^3	2^2	2^1	2^0
Base 8	8^4	8^3	8^2	8^1	8^0
Base 16	16^4	16^3	16^2	16^1	16^0

The largest number in base 10 is a 9, for base 2 it is 1, for base 8 it is 7, for base 16 it is 15. The numbers for base 16 greater than 9 are expressed by letters, i.e., 10 = A, 11 = B, 12 = C, 13 = D, 14 = E, and 15 = F.

The following is a conversion of the base 16 number to the other bases. The number will be $2B7_{16}$

```
    2      B*      7
   ×16     +      +     Base 16   So 2B7₁₆ = 695₁₀
   ───    32     688
   32     ───    ───              *B = 11
          43     695
           ×
          16
          ───
          688
```

The procedure for calculating is to start with the most significant digit and multiply it by the value base used. In this case, the most significant digit is a 2 and the base value is 16. Next, take the result of the multiplication and add this to the next lower digit and then multiply by the digit place value. This was (32+11) x 16 = 688. This procedure continues until the least significant digit is reached. At this point, just add the accumulated value so far with the last digit.

This same process is used for converting any other number of a different base to base 10 number, using the respective base values.

To convert a base 10 number to its base 16 (or any base), the process is as follows: First, the base 10 number is divided by the base number of the base system it is to be converted to. To reconvert 695 base 10 back to base 16, 695/16 = 43 with a remainder of 7. The remainder (7) is the least significant digit of the new base number. Next, 43/16 = 2 with a remainder of 11. 11 is the next digit because we are going to base 16, 11 = B. Since it is less than the base number (16), 2 becomes the most significant digit. So, the converted number is 2B7 base 16.

To convert the base 10 number to base 8, 695/8 = 86 with a remainder of 7, which will be the least significant digit. Now, 86/8 = 10 with a remainder of 6, which is the next digit. Finally, 10/8 = 1 with a remainder of 2, which is the next digit. 1 is left as the most significant digit. So, 695 base 10 = 1267 base 8.

We can reverse this to see if it is correct. Multiply the most significant digit 1 by 8. 1x8=8. Add this to the next digit and multiply by 8, (8+2) x 8 = 80. Add the result to the next digit and multiply by 8, (80+6) x 8 = 688. Now, add the result to the last (least significant) digit, 688 + 7 = 695. So, 695 base 10 does = 1267 base 8.

Performing base 2 calculations is just as simple. Take 21 base 10 and convert to base 2. 21/2 = 10 with a remainder of 1, which is the least significant digit. 10/2 = 5 with a remainder of 0, which will be the next digit. 5/2= 2 with a remainder of 1, the next digit. 2/2 = 1 with a remainder of 0, the next digit. The remaining number will be the next most significant digit. So, 23 base 10 = 10101 base 2.

Reverse this to check: 1x2=2. (2+0) x 2 = 4. (4+1) x 2 = 10. (10+0) x 2 = 20. (20+1) = 21. So, 23 base 10 does equal 10101 base 2.

Flip Flops

Flip flops have one of two stable states. They change states by receiving input pulses. The reset-set flip flop (RS FF) is one of the most basic forms of flip flops made by interconnecting two NAND gates.

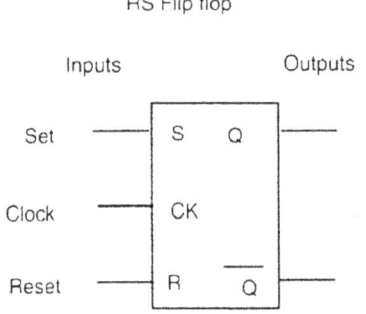

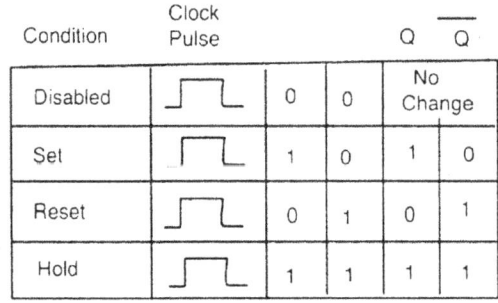

11

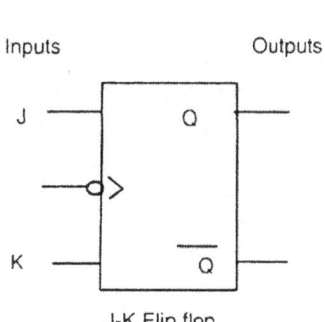

J-K Flip flop

Condition	Clock Pulse	J	K	Q	Q̄
Hold	⎍	0	0	NO Change	
Set	⎍	1	0	1	0
Reset	⎍	0	1	0	1
Toggle	⎍	1	1	Change to Opposite state	

A flip flop with a clock input is called a synchronous device; without a clock input it is called an asynchronous device.

The most common type of flip flop is the J-K flop flip (shown on the previous page). The J + K inputs are data inputs. The arrowhead > at the clock input means that the flip flop is edge triggered. The bubble 0 means that the flip flop is negative edge triggered. Flip flops can be put together to make counters such as:

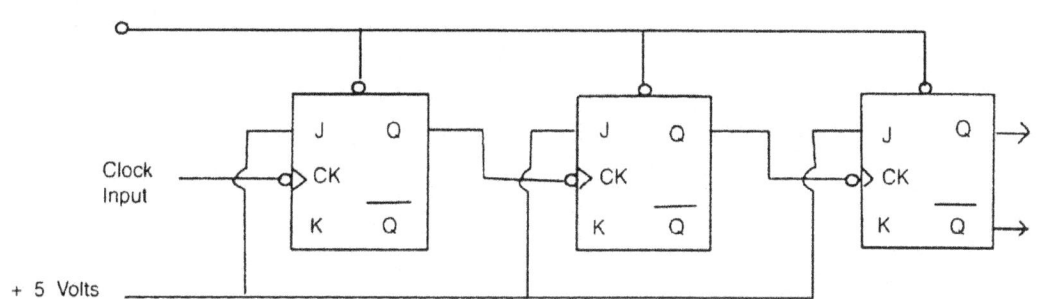

Shift registers also use flip flops in which data is loaded serially (one bit at a time). Once the FF's are loaded with data, they can be shifted left or right (depending upon how they are wired), by clock pulses. Shifting the data to the left or right will either divide by 2 or multiply by 2, depending on which FF has the least significant digit.

The following represent adders which perform arithmetic operations:

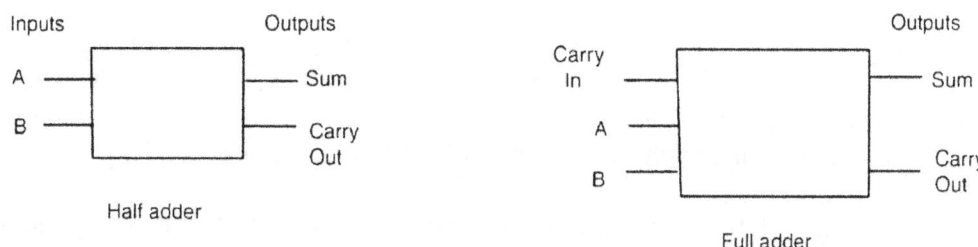

Half adders add binary numbers like the full adder, but do not consider previous carry inputs.

The significance of flip flops is that they can be grouped together to form units of memory, such as RAMs, ROMs, PROMs, and EPROMs. RAM (random access memory) is volatile memory, meaning that when power is turned off, the stored memory is lost. RAM is considered a read-write memory, meaning that you can read data from or write data into the memory. ROM (read-only memory) is non-volatile, meaning that when power is turned off, memory is not lost. ROMs are permanently programmed by the manufacturer and is often called firmware. PROMs (programmable read-only memory) are special ROMs designed to allow the user to program the ROM. EPROMs (erasable programmable read-only memory) are also special ROMs that allow the user to program memories and erase the programs.

Logic Gates

Logic gates use binary inputs. In positive logic, a 1 is a high input and a 0 is a low input. In negative logic, a 1 is a low input and a 0 is a high input.

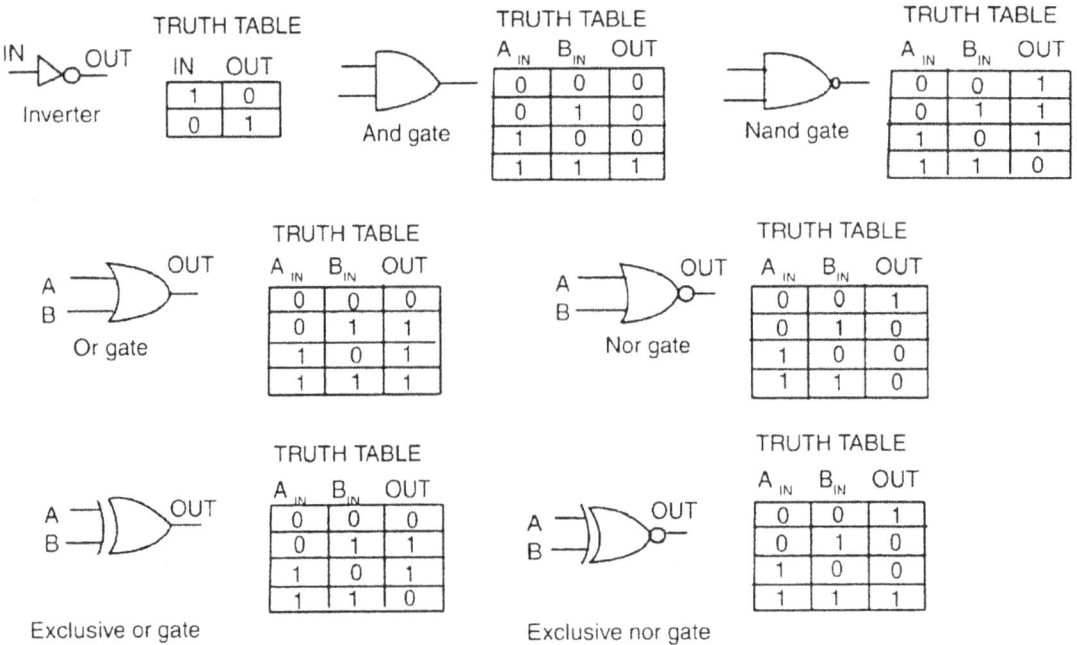

III. OSCILLOSCOPES

Oscilloscopes are used to display instantaneous voltage waveforms in graphic form. The display screen is set up and divided vertically and horizontally in 1 cm divisions. There are 8 vertical divisions in which waveform amplitude is displayed and 10 horizontal divisions in which the time of the wavelength is displayed.

The VOLTS/DIV knob allows the user to select the waveform voltage amplitude in each vertical division to be displayed. The SEC/DIV knob allows the user to select the sweep speed of the waveform in each horizontal division to be displayed.

Proper use of the oscilloscope requires the ability to analyze displayed waveforms by observing the number of divisions a cycle of a given waveform covers both vertically and horizontally.

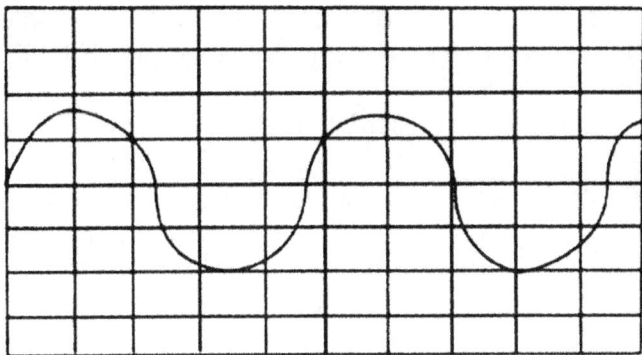

In the waveform shown above, the VOLT/DIV knob is set on 5 volts/div and the SEC/DIV knob is set to 1 msec/div.

Count the number of divisions covered vertically by the waveform, which is 3 1/2 divisions. To get the actual peak-to-peak amplitude of the sinewave, perform the following calculation: 3 1/2 divisions x 5 volts/division = 17.5 volts peak to peak.

Now count the number of divisions covered horizontally by one complete cycle of the waveform, which in this case is 4 1/2 divisions. To find the PRT (pulse repetition time), perform the following calculation: 4 1/2 divisions x .001 sec/division = .0045 seconds. .0045 seconds x msec/.001 sec = 4.5 msec for the PRT.

To find the frequency, simply invert the PRT: Frequency = 1/PRT = 1/.0045 sec = 222.22 cycles/sec or hertz.

The same process could be reversed to find the settings to use on an oscilloscope when you know the amplitude and frequency of a given waveform/signal that you would like to view on the oscilloscope.

<u>Meters</u>

The following are the basics of measuring meters: Always measure current *in series* with the circuit to be measured and always measure voltage in parallel with the circuit.

When performing resistance measurements, always ensure that the component or circuit has no voltage on it and consider whether a specific component may need to be isolated from the rest of the circuit so that the resistance measurement does not follow an alternate path. This can be accomplished by removing one of the *electrical* legs of the component from the circuit. When unsure of the amount of voltage on a circuit to be measured, start with the highest meter setting or range.

When using analog or needle deflection type meters, ensure that you have the proper polarity of leads when checking for DC voltages. One of the most popular analog type multimeters used is the Simpson 260. For copyright reasons, a copy of the meter cannot be given but here are some tips that will work using any analog multimeter. When performing DC measurements, look at the range setting that you have the meter set up for, and find the same corresponding scale on the meter face for proper readings. When performing resistance measurements, read the resistance value on the resistance scale where the needle is deflected to and then multiply this by the resistance range setting. An example of this is with the needle setting on a value of 8 on the resistance scale and the range knob on *RX1000*, then the value of resistance is 8000 ohms.

IV. SCIENTIFIC NOTATION

Scientific notation is a way of expressing large numbers. For example, 100,000,000 ohms could be written as 100×10^6 ohms or 100 megohms. Other prefixes like meg are listed below.

FACTOR	PREFIX	SYMBOL	FACTOR	PREFIX	SYMBOL
10^{12}	tera	T	10^{-2}	centi	c
10^9	giga	G	10^{-3}	milli	m
10^6	mega	M	10^{-6}	micro	μ
10^3	kilo	K	10^{-9}	nano	n
10^2	hecto	h	10^{-12}	pico	p
10^1	deka	da	10^{-15}	femto	f
10^{-1}	deci	d	10^{-18}	atto	a

V. GEARS

Gears are wheels with teeth that are used to transmit mechanical motion from one point to another. The usual configuration is that of two gears meshed together. In this configuration, the larger gear is simply called a *gear* and the smaller gear is called a *pinion*. If the pinion drives the gear, the system is called a speed reducer. If the gear drives the pinion, then the system is called a speed increaser.

When gears are used in increasing or decreasing speeds, they are configured in gear ratios. This allows specific speed changes. For example, for a gear to turn 100 revolutions per minute, if the shaft of the driving motor turns at 1000 revolutions per minute, to achieve the desired speed, it is necessary to use a reducer configuration. This is accomplished by changing the gear ratios. Since gears are made with a certain number of teeth per inch, reducing the number of teeth per inch on the gear attached to the motor shaft to one-tenth of that of the other gear that is being driven would reduce the speed of the driving shaft from 1000 revolutions per minute to 100 revolutions per minute on the driven shaft.

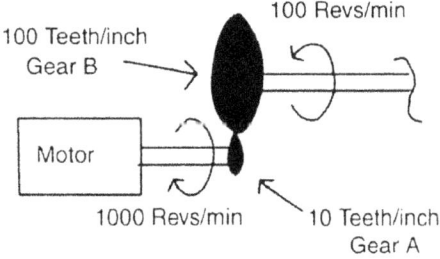

The basic formula for calculating the relationship between the gears and their respective speeds is: Revs/min(gear A) x Teeth/inch (gear A) = Revs/min(gear B) x Teeth/inch(gear B).

When two gears mesh, they turn in opposite directions. Adding a third gear called an idler gear and placing it in-between the two gears will allow them to turn in the same direction. There are four basic types of gear configurations, and they are spur, worm, helical/herringbone, and bevel gears.

Spur gears are the most common type, having straight teeth. They are used to transmit power between two parallel shafts.

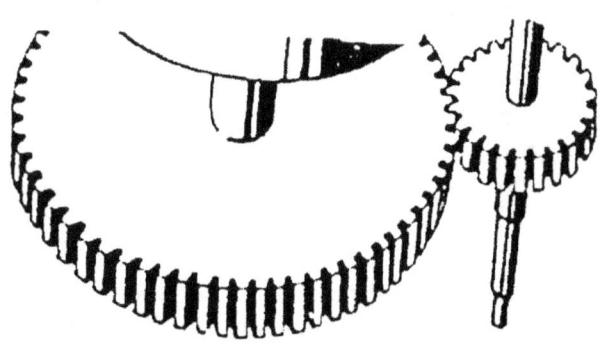

TYPICAL SPUR GEAR

Worm gears having helical teeth are used to transmit power between two shafts whose axis intersect, but not in the same plane. This is probably the most common method of speed reduction, especially in conveyers because the speed of a very fast rotating motor can be greatly reduced.

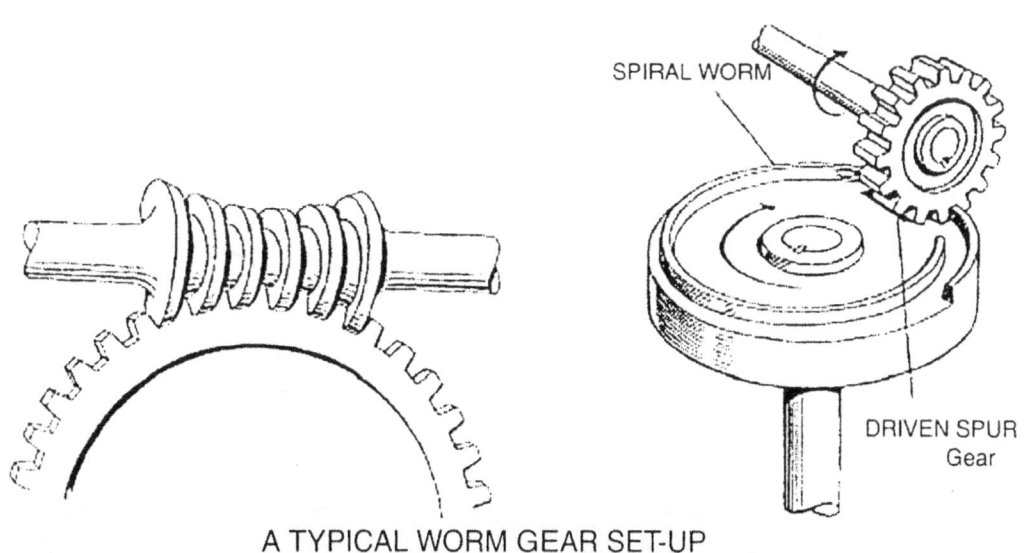

A TYPICAL WORM GEAR SET-UP

Helical/herringbone gears have spiral teeth which allows them to transmit power between two shafts at any angle.

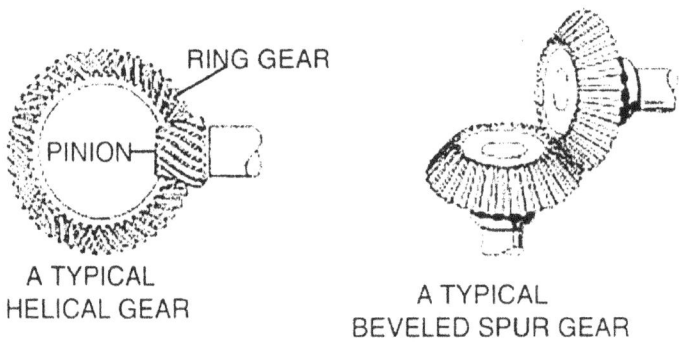

A TYPICAL HELICAL GEAR

A TYPICAL BEVELED SPUR GEAR

<u>Bevel gears</u> are shaped like sections of cones and used to transmit power between shafts whose axis intersect.

Pulleys

Pulleys are wheels used to transmit power such as pulleys used to transmit power from a motor to drive the roller of a conveyer belt. The main feature of a pulley is its ability to change speeds or revolutions per minute. When a pulley drives another pulley with a smaller diameter, the rpms of the second pulley will be greater. This results in a speed increase similar to that in gear systems.

A formula for calculating the circumference around a pulley is: $C = 2\pi r$, where r is the radius of the pulley, and $\pi = 3.14$. Through a series of derivations, the relationship of respective rpms between two connected pulleys is as follows.

Arpms = Brpms x rB/rA where:

    Arpms = revolutions per minute of pulley A
    Brpms = revolutions per minute of pulley B
    rB = radius of pulley B
    rA = radius of pulley A

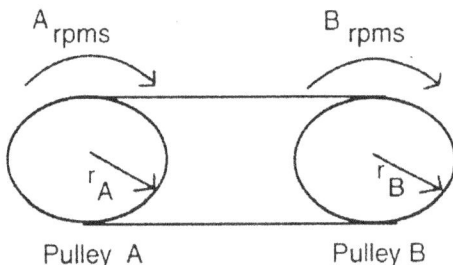

Pulley A   Pulley B

Another use of pulleys is compounding. Compound bows used for archery take advantage of the physics involved in compounding to allow archers to draw bows at high weight pulls with relative ease. For example, to pull up a 100 lb. weight, instead of having to pull with a force of 100 lbs., pulleys can be used to lessen the force required.

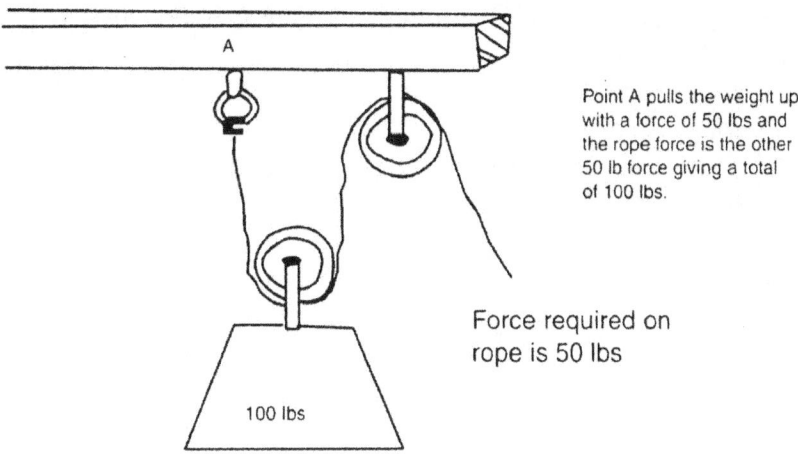

Point A pulls the weight up with a force of 50 lbs and the rope force is the other 50 lb force giving a total of 100 lbs.

Force required on rope is 50 lbs

A pawl is a device used to allow a wheel to turn in one direction and lock the wheel from turning in the other direction. Pawls are commonly found in winching or come-along set-ups.

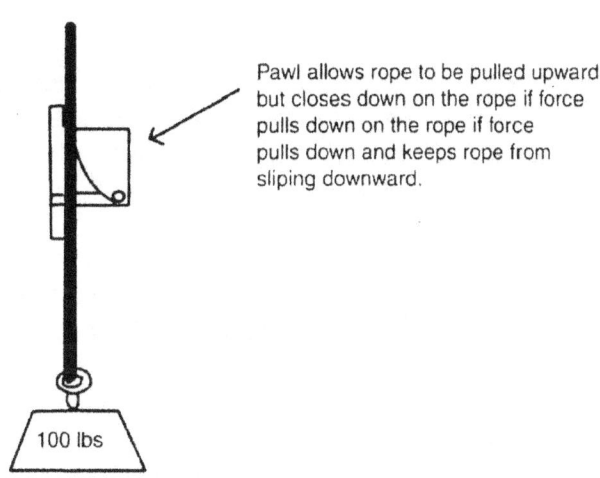

Pawl allows rope to be pulled upward, but closes down on the rope if force pulls down on the rope if force pulls down and keeps rope from sliping downward.

Special coupling is required in power transmissions in order to get mechanical power from one point to another. There are four general types of coupling. The first type is rigid coupling and is rarely used because the shafts must be exactly parallel and, therefore, do not allow for misalignment. The second is flexible coupling which allows for some misalignment although excessive misalignment increases wear. The third type is chain coupling which has been mostly replaced by flexible coupling which requires the most maintenance of all couplings. The last is fluid coupling which uses steel shot as a flow charge. This allows the motor to pick up loads gradually.

Chains should be mounted horizontally or not more than 60 degrees off the horizontal plane. They do allow for the most misalignment. Hook-shaped sprocket teeth show excessive wear. Misalignment may be identified by inspecting for wear on the sides of teeth on the inner surface of roller link plates. The chain sag should not be greater than 2% of the distances from the sprockets, which is 1/4 inch per foot.

A cam is a device connected to a rotating shaft used to convert rotary motion into reciprocal motion.

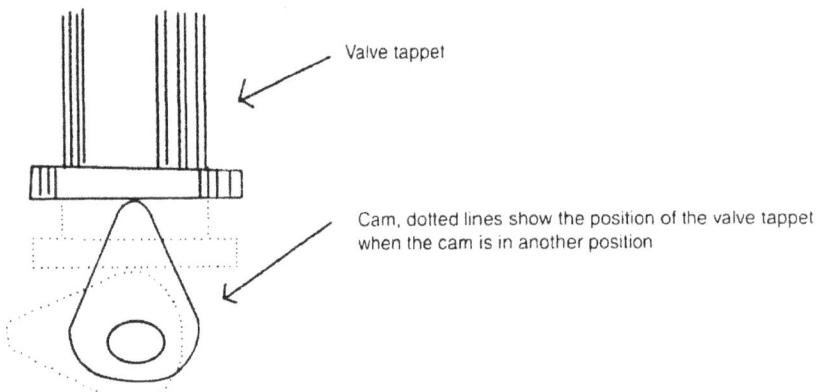

Valve tappet

Cam, dotted lines show the position of the valve tappet when the cam is in another position

Lubricants

Lubrication materials occur in many mediums. Three that will be discussed here are oils, greases, and solids.

Multigrade oils are the most versatile of the oil types. They have additives that allow them to be used in a wide range of temperatures. For example, in an oil labeled 10 w/30, 10 is the SAE viscosity number at 0 degrees Fahrenheit, and the SAE viscosity number at 210 degrees Fahrenheit is 30.

Greases are used in the lubrication of ball or idler bearing systems. Generally speaking, greases are oils that have had thickening agents or *soaps* added. The different kinds of greases are graded from 000, which is a *semi-fluid,* to 6 which is described as being very stiff or thick.

Another type of lubricant is solids. The most common type of solid lubricant is graphite. Another type is molybdenumdisulphide. Solid lubricants are extremely useful as anti-seize compounds to protect rubbing surfaces under high pressures and temperatures from metal pick-up.

BASIC FUNDAMENTALS OF HYDRAULICS AND ELECTRICITY

TABLE OF CONTENTS

	Page
INTRODUCTION	1
HYDRAULICS	1
HYDRAULIC RADIUS	5
ELECTRICITY	18

BASIC FUNDAMENTALS OF HYDRAULICS AND ELECTRICITY

There are similarities between fluids and electricity which help us to understand the fundamental of both. For example, we have the following units of measurement:

	Fluid	Electricity
Pressure	pounds per square inch (psi) or feet of water	electromotive force (emf) E or volts
Flow	gallons per minute (gpm) or cubic feet per second (cfs)	amperes (amp)
Resistance to flow	head loss feet of fluid or psi	resistance (ohms)
Quantity	gallons or cubic feet (gal) or (cf)	kilowatt hours (KWH)

Hydraulics

This is the name given to that branch of science which deals with fluids at rest and in motion. The former is sometimes spoken of as hydrostatics and the latter as hydrodynamics. We are concerned here mainly with water at rest and in motion. Many of the same principles apply to air and gases.

Consideration will be given to water moving or flowing through pipes, channels and pumps and ways of measuring the quantity flowing in a given time. We must be careful of units, the basic ones being:

Length in feet	ft
Area in square feet	sq ft or ft^2
Rate: gallons per minute	gpm.
million gallons per day	mgd
cu ft per second	cfs or sec ft
Weight: 1 gallon of water	8.34 lb
1 cu ft water	62.4 lb
Speed or velocity of flow in feet per second	ft/sec

Head. The precise meaning of the term *head* is the amount of energy possessed by a unit quantity of water at its given location. Ordinarily, the energy is expressed in *foot-pounds,* and the unit quantity of water considered is one pound. The head, then, is expressed in foot-pounds of energy per pound of water, or,

$$\frac{ft \times lb}{lb} = ft$$

Thus, all heads can be expressed in feet. Water may contain energy due to (a) its elevation, (b) its pressure, or (c) its velocity. These energies are called elevation (or static) head, pressure head, and velocity head, respectively. In addition, operators often have occasion to refer to *pump head,* which is the energy required for a pump to move one pound of water, and to *friction head,* which is the energy lost due to friction within the fluid and against the walls of the pipe or channel.

Elevation (or static) head. Elevations must be expressed as the vertical distance from some base level, or reference plane, such as mean sea level, the surface of the ground, or some other arbitrarily chosen level.
Then, for example, water that is 100 ft above the reference plane, has 100 ft-lbs of energy, and its elevation head is 100 ft.

Pressure head. Pressures are expressed in terms of force per unit area, such as pounds per square inch or pounds per square foot. One square foot contains 144 square inches. Therefore, a pressure of 1 lb/in^2 = 144 lb/ft^2, since every square inch is subjected to a force of one pound.
To calculate the energy per pound of water, we must consider the number of pounds of water in a unit volume, which is called the "density" of the water. The density of water is 62.4 lb/ft^3. Then if the pressure of the water is 1 lb/in^2 (often written 1 psi), the "pressure head" is

$$\frac{144 \text{ lb/ft}^2}{62.4 \text{ lb/ft}^3} = 2.3 \text{ ft}$$

or
1 psi = 2.3 ft pressure head

By the same kind of calculation, a water pressure of 40 psi equals

$$\frac{40 \times 144 \text{ lb/ft}^2}{62.4 \text{ lb/ft}^2} = 92.3 \text{ ft pressure head}$$

or
40 X 2.3 = 92.3 ft pressure head

Velocity head. The energy of motion is called kinetic energy, and is calculated by the relationship

$$\text{Energy} = \frac{mv^2}{2g}$$

where m represents the mass of the moving object, v its velocity, and g the force which gravity exerts on a mass of one pound.

In everyday speech, we are accustomed to expressing both force and mass in pounds. However, this causes confusion when energy calculations are attempted, because the force exerted by gravity is not numerically equal to the mass in pounds. That is to say, force and mass cannot properly be expressed in the same units.

One way of avoiding this difficulty is to speak of the force of gravity in terms of the acceleration it produces when it acts upon a unit mass. One of the fundamental laws of physics is that force equals mass times acceleration. Thus, the force on a unit mass of one pound is numerically equal to the acceleration.

Acceleration is the rate at which velocity changes. If an automobile goes from zero miles per hour to sixty miles per hour in two minutes, we can say that its average change of speed was thirty miles per hour in each minute, or thirty miles per hour per minute. Likewise, if water moving ten feet per second speeds up to fifteen feet per second, and the time required for the change of speed is one second, we could say that it accelerated five feet per second per second. Accelerations are often expressed in feet per second. The units can then be written ft/sec. This is equivalent to writing $\frac{ft}{sec \times sec}$ or $\frac{ft}{sec^2}$

When gravity acts upon a free-falling body, it produces an acceleration of 32.2 ft/sec^2. This value of g can be used in the equation for calculating velocity head. If we consider, for example one pound of water moving with a velocity of 10 ft/sec, its velocity head is calculated as follows:

$$\text{Energy} = \frac{1 \text{ lb} \times 10 \text{ ft/sec} \times 10 \text{ ft/sec}}{2 \times 32.2 \text{ ft/sec}^2} = 1.5 \text{ ft-lb}$$

$$\text{Velocity head} = \frac{1.5 \text{ ft-lb}}{1 \text{ lb}} = 1.5 \text{ ft}$$

In the first of these two equations we multiplied by the weight of the water. In the second we divided by the weight of the water. Since these two operations cancel each other, the velocity head can be calculated by leaving out the weight in the first place:

$$\text{Velocity head} = \frac{v^2}{2g}$$

Friction head. Friction head equals the loss of energy due to friction within the liquid and friction against the walls of the pipe or channel. When we are dealing with water, the friction within the liquid is relatively small, and most of the energy is lost due to friction against the walls. Therefore, the friction loss depends mostly upon the characteristics of the material of which the pipe or channel is made and its surface smoothness. The usual procedure for estimating friction head losses is to use a table in an engineering handbook which gives directly the friction loss per foot of a particular kind of pipe or channel.

Pump head. The pump head equals the ft-lb of energy given to each pound of water passing through the pump.

Pumping. Pumps are used to move liquids to a higher level or to increase the rate of flow. Figure (1) and Figure (2) show two typical pumping conditions. To understand these figures it is necessary to know that in a liquid at rest the pressure at any point is equal to the weight of the liquid above the point, plus the weight of the atmosphere above the surface of the liquid. Both, must be expressed in the same units.

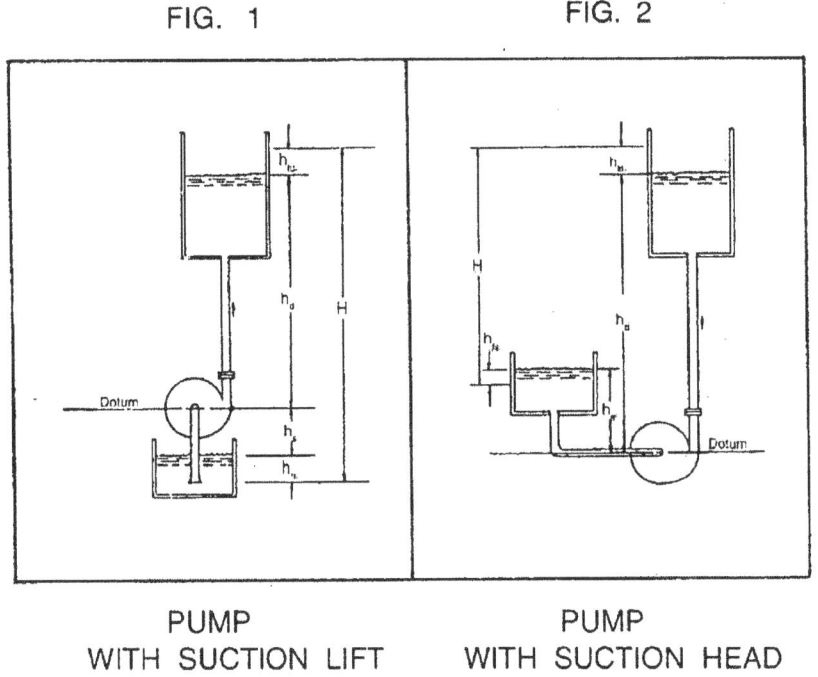

FIG. 1 — PUMP WITH SUCTION LIFT

FIG. 2 — PUMP WITH SUCTION HEAD

These units are usually pounds per square inch (psi) or feet of water. Since most pumping problems involve difference in pressure, the atmospheric pressure may be neglected and gauge pressures (psig) or height in feet may be used. Total head in feet at a point can be expressed as the height of a column of water whose weight would produce a certain pressure at that point. Psi X 2.31 = head in feet.

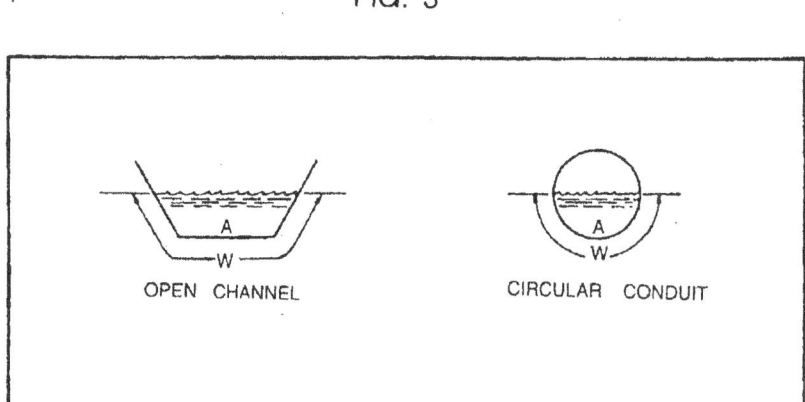

FIG. 3

OPEN CHANNEL   CIRCULAR CONDUIT

HYDRAULIC RADIUS

For Figure 1— Pump operating with a suction lift:

$$H = h_d + h_s + h_{fd} + h_{fa} + \frac{V_d^2}{2g} \quad \frac{V_s^2}{2g}$$

For Figure 2 — Pump operating with suction head:

$$H = h_d + h_s + h_{fd} + h_{fa} + \frac{V_d^2}{2g} \quad \frac{V_s^2}{2g}$$

Where —
- H = Total head in feet (formerly called total dynamic head) at which the pump operates.
- h_d = Static discharge head in feet, or the vertical distance between the pump datum and liquid surface in the receiving tank. The pump datum is at the center line for horizontal pumps and at the entrance eye of the impeller for vertical pumps.
- $h.$ = Static suction head or lift in feet or vertical distance between pump datum and liquid surface in the suction well.
- h_{fd} = Friction head in discharge in feet or the head necessary to overcome friction in valves, fittings, etc. in the discharge piping.
- h_{fs} = Friction head in suction in feet
- g = 32.2 ft/sec² = Acceleration due to gravity.

$\frac{V_d^2}{2g}$ and $\frac{V_s^2}{2g}$ discharge nozzle and suction nozzle of the pump. When the nozzles are of the same diameter these values are equal and cancel out. Velocity head represents energy which the pump must deliver to the liquid but which is not measured by a pressure gage. It is the head required to give to the liquid the velocity "V" in feet per second.

The relationship between the volume of water flowing per unit of time, the velocity of the moving water and the size of pipe or channel through which the flow takes place may be expressed by the equation:

$$Q = AV$$

Where
- Q = rate of flow or volume per unit time (usually expressed as cubic ft/sec (cfs)
- A = Area through which water is flowing, measured at right angles in the direction of flow (usually expressed in sq ft)
- V = Average velocity of flow or distance traveled per unit of time (usually expressed as ft/sec)

There are three general types of problems using the equation $Q = AV$. These are as follows:

1. The water in an open channel has been observed to flow a distance of 180 feet in 2 minutes. The dimensions of the channel are 2 feet wide and 18 inches deep. Compute the rate of flow

   $$V = \frac{180}{2 \text{ min}} = \frac{90 \text{ ft}}{\text{min}} = \frac{1.5 \text{ ft}}{\text{sec}}$$

   $$A = 2 \text{ ft} \times 18 \text{ in} \times \frac{\text{ft}}{12 \text{ in}} = 3.0 \text{ sq ft}$$

   then

   $$Q = AV = 3.0 \text{ sq ft} \times \frac{1.5 \text{ ft}}{\text{sec}} = 4.5 \text{ cfs}$$

2. A meter shows water flowing through a 12 inch diameter pipe at the rate of 2 mgd. To determine the velocity of the water

   $$Q = \frac{2,000,000 \text{ gal}}{\text{day}} \times \frac{\text{cu ft}}{7.5 \text{ gal}} \times \frac{\text{day}}{24 \text{ hr}} \times \frac{\text{hr}}{60 \text{ min}} \times \frac{\text{min}}{60 \text{ sec}} = 3.08 \text{ cfs}$$

   $$A = \pi r^2 = 3.1416 \times 6 \text{ in} \times 6 \text{ in} \times \frac{\text{sq ft}}{144 \text{ sq ft}} = 0.79 \text{ sq ft}$$

   then $V = Q/A = \dfrac{3.08 \text{ cu ft}}{0.79 \text{ sq ft} \times \text{sec}} = 3.9 \dfrac{\text{ft}}{\text{sec}}$

3. Baffles are to be placed in a coagulation tank so that the velocity of flow between baffles is 0.3 ft/sec. The depth of flow in the tank is 8 feet and the rate of flow through the tank is 2 mgd. Find the distance, w between baffles.

   $$Q = 2 \text{ mgd} \times 1.55 \frac{\text{cfs}}{\text{mgd}} = 3.08 \text{ cfs}$$

   V = 0.3 ft/sec
   let the distance between baffles equal w

   then $A = 8 \times w = \dfrac{Q}{V} = 3.08 \dfrac{\text{cu ft}}{\text{sec}} \times \dfrac{\text{sec}}{0.3 \text{ ft}}$

   $$W = \frac{3.08 \text{ cu ft / sec}}{8 \text{ ft} \times 0.3 \text{ ft / sec}} = 1.28 \text{ ft}$$

Pipe Friction. The h_{fd} and h_{fs} in the preceding paragraphs are those portions of the total head necessary to overcome friction between the fluid and the walls of the suction and discharge piping. The values of these terms depend upon the length of the pipeline, its diameter, the velocity of the flowing liquid and the condition of the internal walls of the pipe, usually called the roughness factor. These influences are expressed in the formula

h_f = Friction head = $f \dfrac{L}{d} \dfrac{V^2}{2g}$

Where f = roughness factor
       L = length of pipe
       d = diameter

$\dfrac{V^2}{2g}$ = velocity head

Tables are available for the value of f, which varies with both V and d in this formula. The value of f is fractional, varying from .04 for small V and d to .01 for large values of V and d. Another formula derived from this basic one expresses the roughness factor as a whole number known as the C value in the Hazen & Williams formula. Tables and a special slide rule have been developed for solving pipe problems by this formula. The value of C varies from 140 for very smooth large pipe to a low of 40 or less for badly corroded or dirty pipe. See Figure 4 (Flow Chart for value "C" equals 100)

FIG. 4

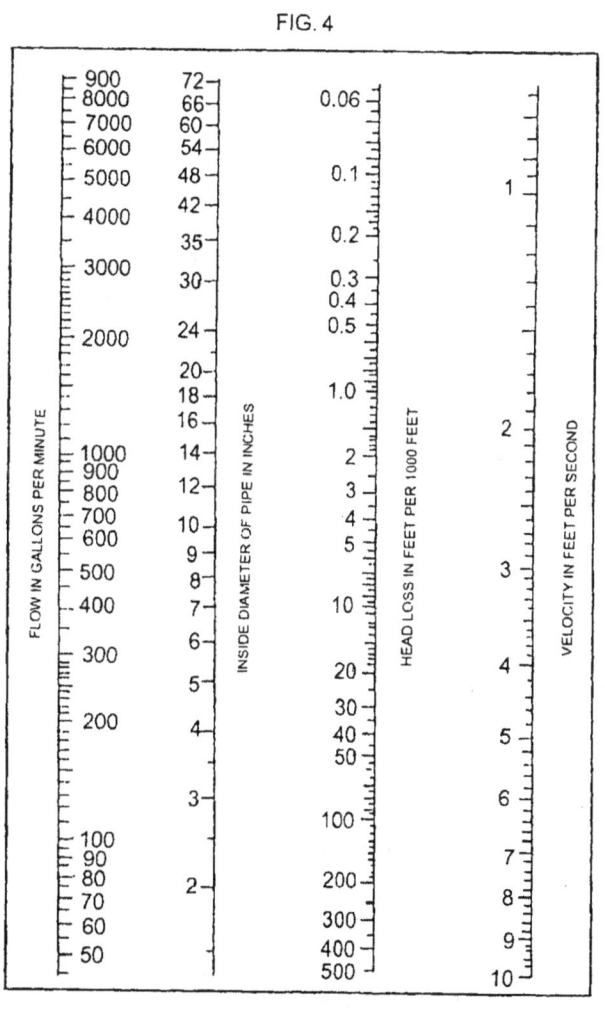

FLOW CHART
"C" 100
Based on the Hazen-Williams Formula

FIG. 5

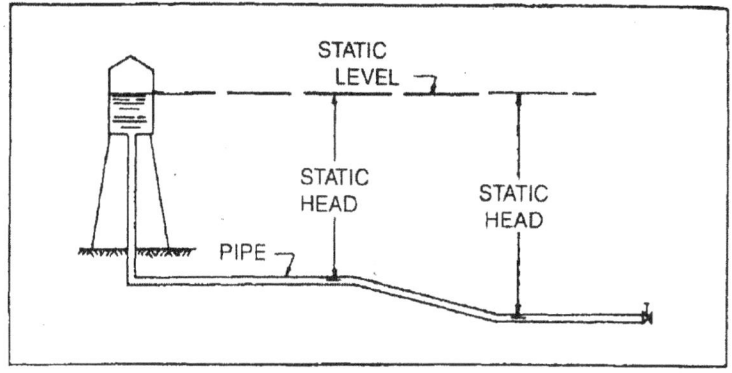

STATIC HEAD

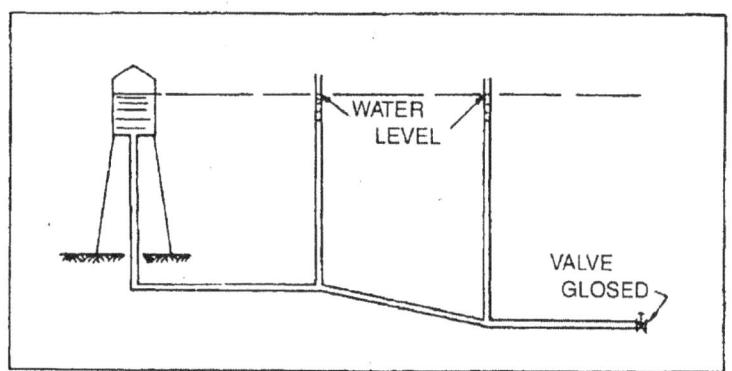

WATER LEVEL, NO FLOW IN PIPE

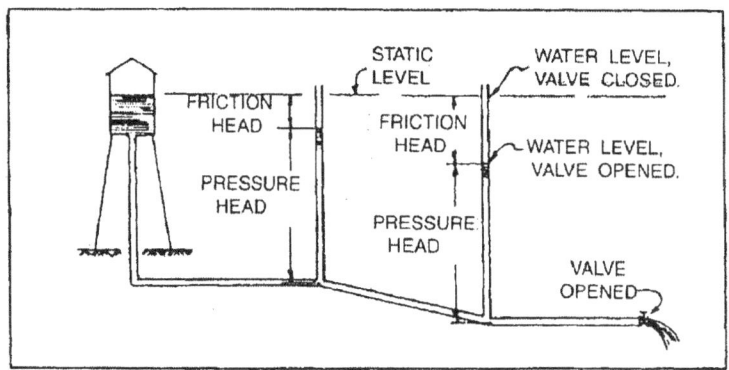

PRESSURE HEAD

If vertical open pipes are attached in a pipe line as shown in Figure 6, the water level in the pipes will stand at a level even with the elevation of the water in the storage tank. If the outlet valve is opened to permit water to flow, the level of the water in the vertical pipes will drop. The drop in the level or loss in head is the "friction head" and represents the energy lost by friction of the water flowing through the pipe.

Power Requirements for Pumping. Work must be done to move liquid against the total heads (H) indicated in Figures 8 and 9. The unit of work is the foot pound which is the amount of work or energy required to lift one pound a vertical distance of one foot. The common unit of power or rate of doing work is horsepower (hp). One horsepower is equal to 33,000 ft. lbs. per minute. In electrical units, one horsepower is equivalent to 746 watts.

The power required to drive a pump can be computed as follows:
Work done by the pump (or water horsepower) = Whp

$$Whp = \frac{lbs. \text{ of water raised per minute} \times H}{33,000}$$

$$= \frac{gpm \times 8.34 \times H}{33,000} = \frac{gpm \times H}{3,960}$$

Example: The sum of the elevation, pressure, velocity and friction heads is 100 ft. What would be the work done by the pump or the horsepower required (water horsepower) if 50 gallons per minute is pumped?

$$Whp = \frac{gal/min \times lbs/gal \times ft\,lbs/lb}{ft\text{-}lbs/min}$$

$$= 1.26 \text{ horsepower}$$

Since all the power delivered by the driving unit cannot be converted to useful work, the ratio between output and input is called pump efficiency.
Power required to drive the pump, or "brake horsepower" is computed by this formula:

$$bhp = \frac{whp}{pump\ eff} = \frac{gpm \times 8.33 \times H}{33,000 \times pump\ eff} = \frac{gpm \times H}{3960 \times pump\ eff}$$

If the efficiency (eff) of the pump is 65%

$$\frac{1.26}{0.65} = 1.94 \text{ horsepower must be delivered to the pump.}$$

Again since motors are not 100% efficient

$$Motor\ hp = \frac{whp}{pump\ eff \times motor\ eff}$$

$$= \frac{gpm \times H}{3960 \times pump\ eff \times motor\ eff}$$

If the motor efficiency is 80%

$$\frac{1.26}{0.65 \times 0.80} = 2.425$$

horsepower must be delivered to the motor in order to pump 50 gpm against a total head of 100 feet.

Flow in Open Channels. Flow in open conduits and in partially filled pipes is affected by the same factors as in pipes flowing full. These factors determine the slope required for an open channel to maintain a certain flow and velocity. The velocity, is actually determined by the slope of the water surface, but this is usually also the slope of the bottom of the channel and the water flows at a constant depth. The slope of the water surface is called the hydraulic gradient. The friction between water and the conduit walls depends upon the roughness of the surface, but the formula for it is different because the liquid now has a free surface and the length of contact depends upon the shape of the channel and the depth of flow. These factors are combined in the " hydraulic radius," which is found by dividing the cross-sectional area of the flowing water by the distance around that area along the walls of the channel. This distance is called the "wetted perimeter" of the channel (see Figure 3). Thus,

Hyd Rad $r = \dfrac{A}{W}$ feet (figure 3)

From these considerations, there has been developed the Chezy formula:

$v = C\sqrt{rs}$ feet per sec

where C = coefficient based on roughness, slope and value of r.

s = slope of the hydraulic gradient or water surface in open channels, usually expressed as ft per foot or ft per thousand feet. Thus, a slope of .004 indicates a drop of four feet in a thousand foot length.

The two principal formulas for determining C, the Kutter and the Manning formulas, depend largely upon values of "n" which is the coefficient of friction. These values have become quite well known for various types of surfaces and materials. Thus n=.013 is commonly used for design of vitrified tile pipes and for large diameter pre-cast concrete pipes.

Tables and diagrams have been published from which velocities, rates of flow and slopes can be determined for various diameters of pipes and values of "n".

Weirs. There are numerous ways of measuring flowing water, but three devices most commonly used are weirs, Venturi meters, and Parshall flumes.

The weir consists of rectangular opening or V notch opening with sharp edges. The weir is set vertically so that the flow passes over it tnd falls away from it.

FIG. 6

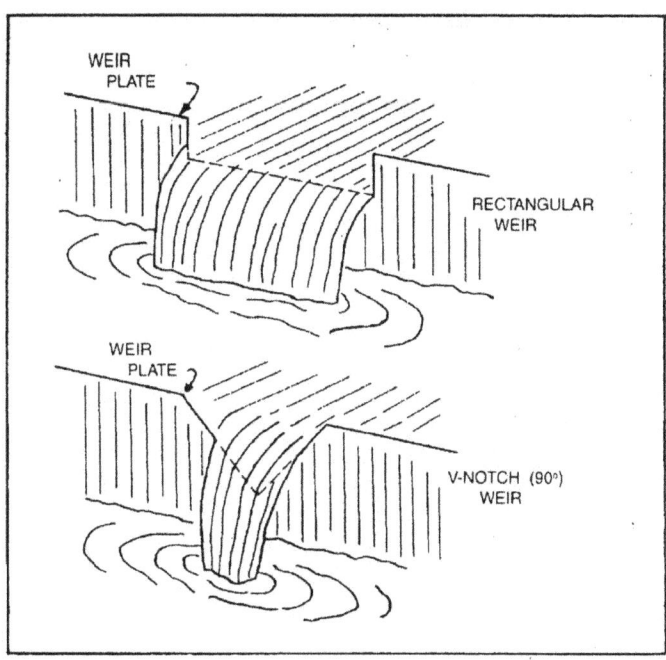

WEIRS

It is only necessary to measure the height of water above the crest of the weir at a point sufficiently upstream which avoids the curve of the water surface over the weir. In placing a weir, two points must be considered. First, the weir should be installed in the channel so that the velocity of the water approaching the weir is relatively low. Second, the "head" on the weir is not the depth of water as it passes over the weir proper but is the difference in elevation between the edge of the weir and the water upstream a short distance. In Figure 7 both of these points are illustrated. By using the head measurement the flow is determined from the formula:

Rate of flow $Q = 3.33 \, L \, h\sqrt{h}$ cfs (for a suppressed weir) and

$Q = 3.33 \, (L - \frac{h}{5}) \, h \cdot \sqrt{h}$ cfs (for a contracted weir)

where h = the height of horizontal water surface above crest of weir, L= horizontal length of weir.

The V notch weir is more accurate than the rectangular weir for small flows. For a 90 degree notch, the formula is: (Figure 8)

$Q = Ch^2 \sqrt{h}$ cfs where

C is a coefficient depending upon the material of the weir and the range of head. Values of C are given in handbooks for various materials and heads. The V notch weir is suitable for measuring flows from 10 to 3,500 gpm.

Another formula which may be used with a V notch weir with

90° angle is

$Q = 2.5h^{5/2}$

where Q = rate of discharge in cfs
h = "head" on weir in feet (Figure 8)

Using the chart. (Figure 8)
If h is measured to be 0.20 feet then Q = .045cfs
= 21 gpm

FIG. 7

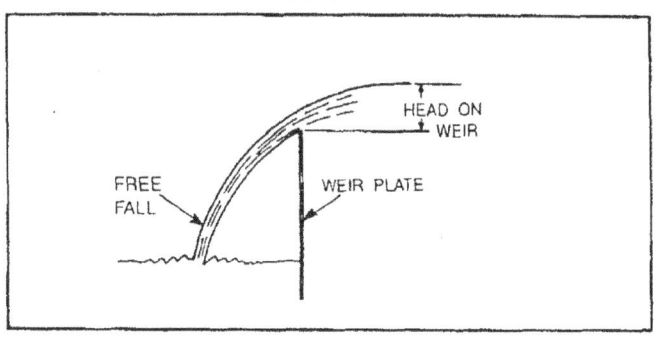

HEAD ON WEIR

FIG. 8

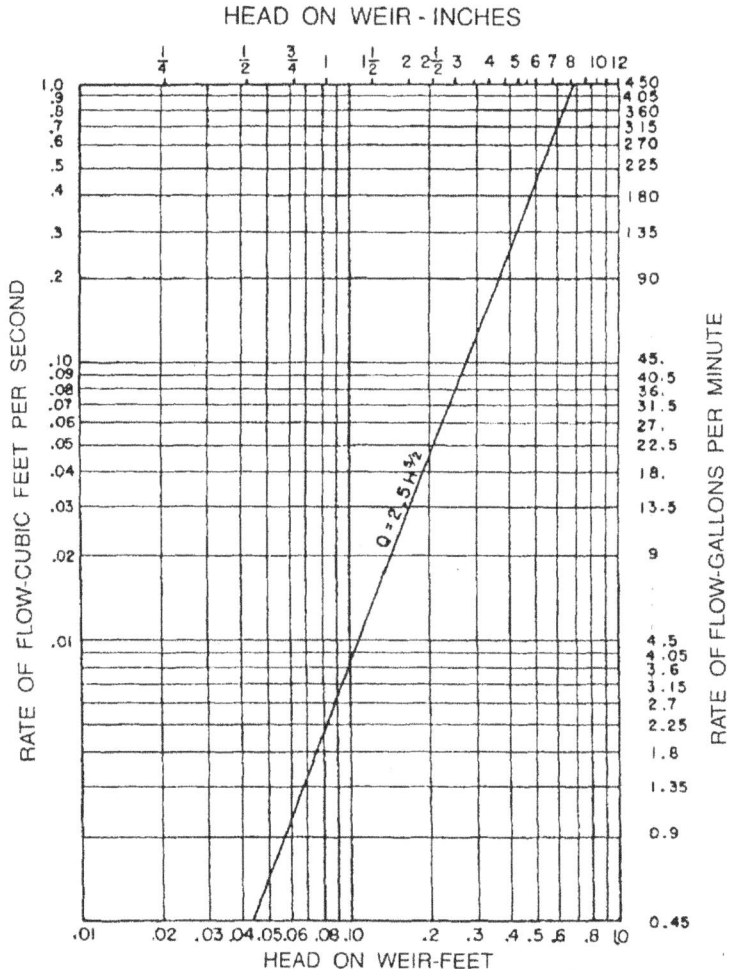

90° V-NOTCH WEIR FORMULA-Q=2.5H5/2

Venturi Meter. This type of flow measuring device is installed in a pipe line and consists of a throat carefully machined to a given inside diameter, a converging section which tapers from the pipe diameter to the throat and a diverging section from the throat to the pipe diameter. (See Figure 9) Taps are provided for measuring pressure head at points just before convergence and at the throat. The only measurement necessary to compute the flow is the difference in pressure head between the two tap points. Figure 10 shows graphically how pressure and velocity heads change in the Venturi Meter.

Parshall Flume. This type of flow measuring device was developed for measuring irrigation water in open channels where there may be debris and silt and where little loss of head can be permitted.

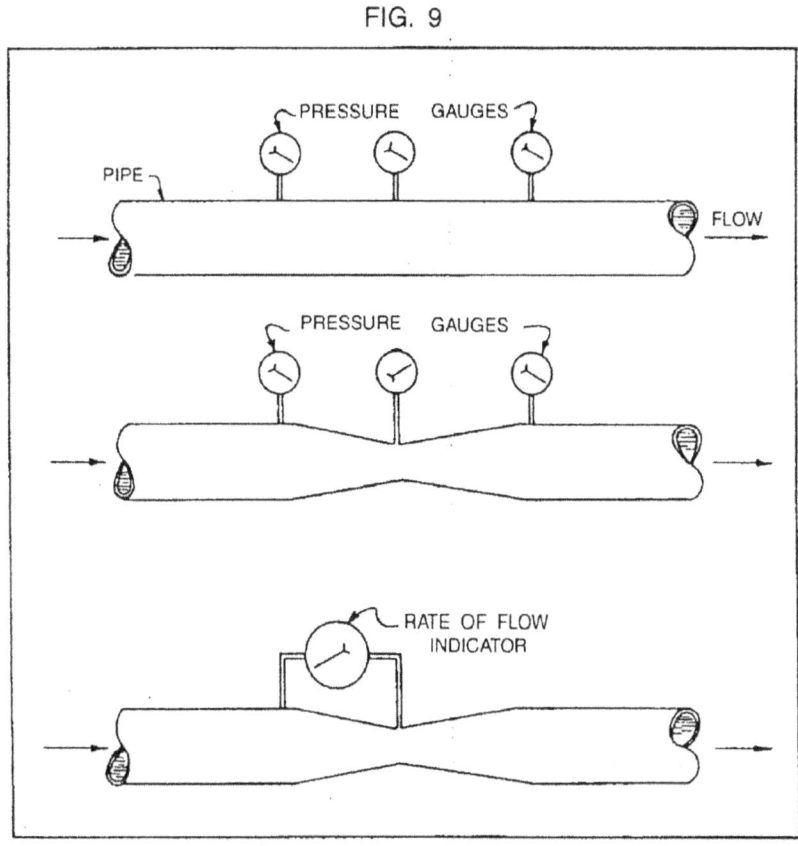

FIG. 9

VENTURI TUBE

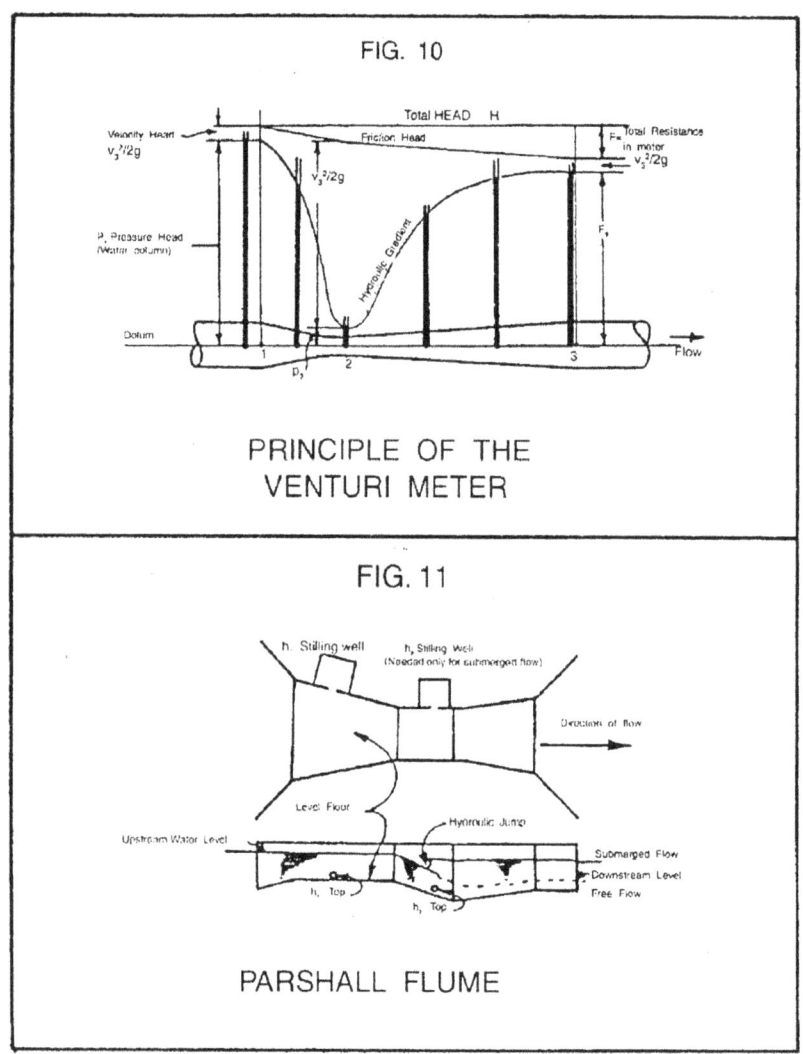

FIG. 10 PRINCIPLE OF THE VENTURI METER

FIG. 11 PARSHALL FLUME

In principle, the flume is similar to the Venturi meter. It has an inlet section with sides converging slowly to a throat of fixed dimensions and an outlet section diverging more rapidly to the original channel width. For the usual non-submerged condition only measurement of the depth of water at a fixed distance upstream from the throat is necessary to determine the flow. The flume may be constructed of almost any building material. For greatest accuracy the throat is often made to accurate dimensions from corrosion resistant metal. Figure 11 illustrates the Parshall Flume.

Magnetic Flow Meter. Bach of the previously described flow measuring devices involves an appreciable loss of head. A new development consists of a non-magnetic tube of the same internal diameter as the pipe line across which a magnetic field is established. Water flowing through the magnetic field produces a voltage proportional to the velocity. This voltage is converted by electrical and mechnical means to indicate and record the rate of flow.

An important operating and maintenance requirement of any flow measuring device is that pressure connecting stilling wells, floats and float tubes must be kept clean.

Rate of Flow Controllers. These are used to maintain flows at constant rates. Generally, all of the newer models depend on the Venturi principle to control a movable diaphragm or a pilot valve. This in turn actuates a main valve so as to control the size of an opening so that the desired amount of water is passed. Figure 12 shows a section through one type of controller. Actually this particular type of controller has two valves on the vertical stem and two valve seats but, for simplification, only one has been shown.

FIG. 12

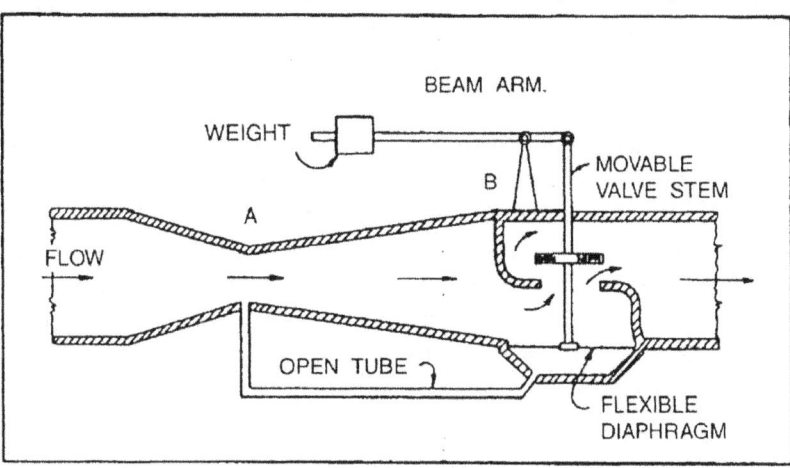

RATE OF FLOW CONTROLLER

The weight is placed at the desired point on the beam arm which corresponds to a certain rate of flow through the valve. At this particular rate of flow the unit pressure at point "A" will be less than the unit pressure at point "B". The unit pressure at point A is transferred, by means of the small open tube, to the compartment below the flexible diaphragm. The downward total pressure on the diaphragm is then greater than the upward total pressure. This results in a tendency for the valve stem to move downward. This tendency is counteracted by the weight at the proper location on the beam arm. At the desired rate of flow everything is in balance.

Pumps. Pumps have many uses in waterworks practice. Though there are many types, practically all water pumps may be classified into two general categories: displacement pumps and velocity pumps.

Displacement pumps employ some mechanical means (plungers, pistons, gears or cams) for forcing specific volumes of water through the units. Velocity pumps impart a high velocity to water and convert the velocity head into pressure head which forces the water through the apparatus.

Either type of pump raises the pressure on inlet side to a higher pressure on the outlet side. The specific means for bringing this about are quite different for the two types. Displacement type pumps, when operating at a particular speed, will take specific unit volumes of water and mechanically force the water out of the pump at a certain rate without regard to conditions beyond the pumping unit. When the resistance to flow beyond the pump is increased, the pressure will be increased. The only limit is the available horsepower and the physical strength of the discharge pipe or the pump. In other words, if something goes wrong on the discharge side of the pump to stop the flow, something may have to "give" and serious damage may result.

This is not the case with a velocity pump. A velocity pump merely causes the water to move with a very high velocity within the pump, usually in a circular direction. Under most conditions the amount of water which passes through the pump depends upon the resistance to flow on the discharge side. If the resistance is too great, for example if a valve is closed, the pump will continue to operate. This will produce the maximum pressure obtainable from that particular pump and speed of operation, but no wa.ter will pass through the pump. Probably no damage will result unless the pump is allowed to run until it over heats.

Displacement pumps may be subdivided into two general types-reciprocating and rotary. The reciprocating type, equipped with either plungers or pistons, includes direct acting, single or duplex, steam pumps, crank and flywheel pumps, and plunger pumps. Rotary pumps may be either cam, screw or gear types.

Velocity pumps may be subdivided into several general types including centrifugal, propeller, mixed flow, and turbine units.

Displacement pumps have certain advantages over velocity types. In displacement pumps the quantity of liquid delivered does not vary with the discharge head; they are easily primed; many act like air pumps and prime themselves when the suction head is low. They will operate smoothly on high suction lifts up to 25 feet or so. For high heads and small quantities the reciprocating pump is probably still the best. For many applications, the velocity pump, particularly the centrifugal pump, has displaced the reciprocating pump. Advantages of velocity pumps are lower initial cost, generally higher efficiency and easier installation and maintenance.

FIG. 13

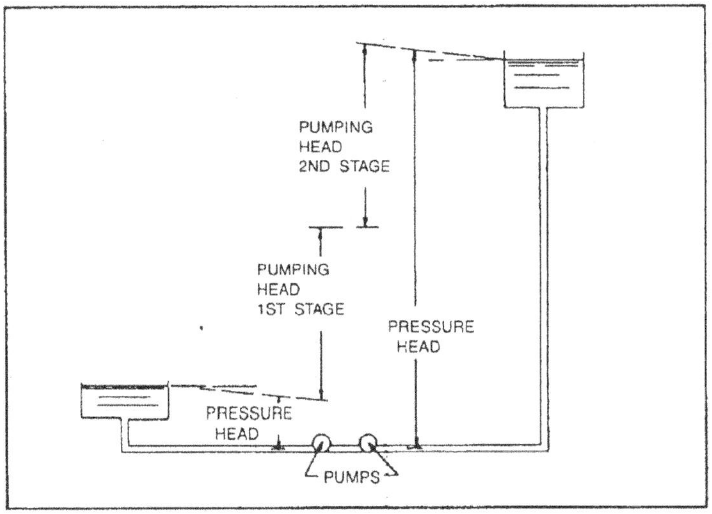

TWO STAGE PUMPING

Centrifugal Pumps. In the centrifugal pump, pressure is developed almost entirely by centrifugal force. Water enters at the center of an impeller which is rotated at high speed. Pressure is exerted and water moves to the outside. A specially shaped casing around the impeller discharges the water through a single opening to discharge line. There are various types of impellers. These include the open type which is commonly" used for pumping sewage and the closed type which is commonly used for pumping clear water. The water may enter at one side of the impeller in the side suction pump or on both sides in the double suction pump. Two or more pumps are used in stages when pumping against high heads. More than one stage can be obtained by using several impellers mounted on a single shaft. Also, two individual pumps can be mounted on a single shaft, driven by one motor, when the head conditions are high. The application of a multistage layout is illustrated in Figure 13.

Centrifugal pumps may be operated with suction lifts. With all but minimum lifts, priming arrangements may be required.

The performance and operating characteristics are given on a pump curve sheet supplied by the manfacturer for each pump. On Figure 14 the curves show the discharge in gallons per minute (gpm) of the pump at various heads, the pump efficiency under different head-discharge conditions and the brake horsepower under various head-discharge conditions. As the head increases the discharge decreases until the shut-off head is reached.

FIG. 14

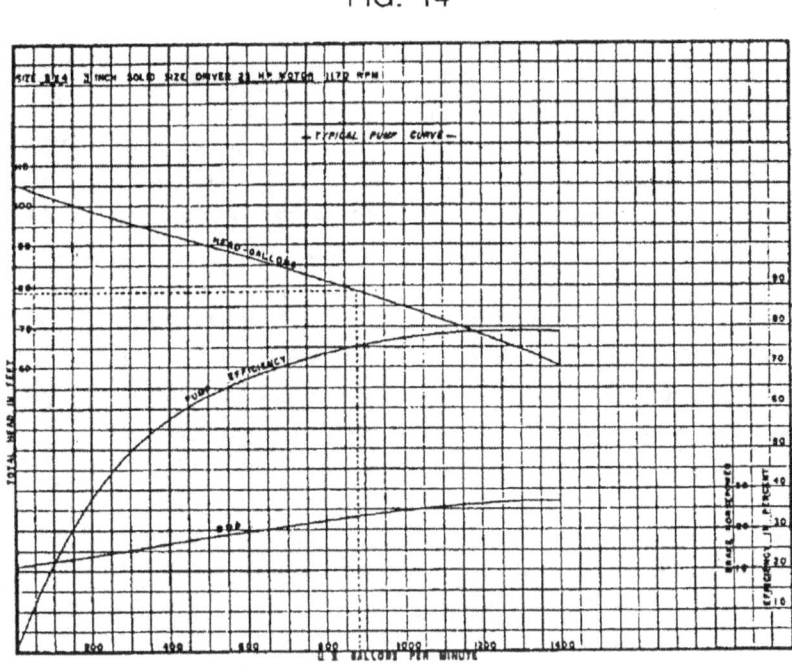

TYPICAL PUMP CURVE

On the pump curves, Figure 14, dotted lines indicate how values can be read from these curves. The pump for which these curves were prepared, when operated at 1170 revolutions per minute (rpm), will deliver 880 gpm at a total head of 79 feet. The brake horsepower (bhp) of the pump is 23 and the pump efficiency 75%. For a motor with an efficiency of 92 percent, the mhp (motor horsepower) should be 25. (Refer to power requirement for pumping). The shutoff head at which no water is delivered is 105 feet.

Large centrifugal pumps usually operate at slow speeds to minimize wear and maintenance costs.

The other velocity pumps have, in general, similar operating characteristics. They may vary considerably in construction and have different applications to water pumping problems. Propeller types are usually limited to low heads and the turbine type, with several stages, is most often used as a deep well pump.

18
Electricity

Electrical Units. The volt, as indicated in the introduction to this chapter, expresses electrical pressure just as feet, head or psi expresses water pressure. It is represented by the symbol "E", or sometimes emf, the abbreviation for electro-motive force.

For years, standard voltages have been 110, 220, 440, 2,200, 4,400 and 13,200. In water plants the voltage seldom exceeds 440. Higher voltages are used primarily for transmission lines. In some places the 110 and 220 standards have been replaced by 120 and 208. High voltages require proper equipment to prevent leaks (short circuits), and must be respected for personal-safety. Even pressures as low as 110 volts can be fatal.

Proper equipment should be used for the voltage furnished. If the average voltage is 120 on lighting circuits, then 120 and not 110 volt lamps should be used. They will last about three times as long.

For motors over 50 hp, voltages in excess of 440 is desirable. For 5 to 50 hp motors, economy dictates the use of 220 and 440 volts.

The ampere (amp) in electricity expresses the rate of flow, as gpm expresses water flows. In equations, the ampere is represented by I. Just as large pipes are required for large flows of water, large wire sizes are required for hea.vy amperages to keep down the losses due to resistance. Voltage drop due to resistance is similar to head loss due to friction in a pipe line.

Every electrical device has a current rating depending upon its design and resistance to flow. In motors the current varies with the load. Wires, fuses and switches are rated as to the current which they may safely carry. These ratings are fixed by a National Electric Code and should not be exceeded. An appliance rated for 25 amps should be protected by a fuse of that capacity to act as a safety valve. When carrying more than their rated capacity, wires and appliances overheat and may burn out or cause fires.

The ohm is the unit of electrical resistance. In electrical circ-cuits the loss of voltage, voltage drop, or loss in pressure is proportional to the resistance and the rate of current flow. Thus we have the simple relation known as Ohm's Law: $E = RI$. Values of resistance R for unit lengths or conductors of various sizes and materials are found in handbooks.

Direct and Alternating Currents. If the current flows first in one and then the other direction, it is known as alternating current and the number of times per second that it flows in each direction determines the number of cycles. A current that flows in any one direction 60 times per second is called 60 cycle. This is the standard for alternating current in this country.

Transformers are used to increase or decrease voltage. They consist of two stationary coils of wire insulated from each other but wound around a common iron core. Current flowing through the primary coil induces a current in the secondary with a voltage related to the number of turns of wire on the primary and secondary coils.

The Watt (W) is the unit of electrical power (P) and is most commonly used as a thousand watts or the kilowatt (KW). The mechanical unit of power or horsepower (HP) is equivalent to 746 watts. For rough computation it can be remembered that horsepower is approximately equivalent to three-quarters of a KW. Since the efficiency of many small motors is about 75%, one kilowatt in-put is roughly equivalent to one HP out-put.

For direct current:
$P = EI$. By substitution for E,
$P = RI^2$, or by substitution for I

$$P = \frac{E^2}{R}$$

From these expressions it can be seen that power varies directly with both current and voltage if resistance is not considered, but as the square of either one when resistance is considered.

The "kilowatt hour" is the unit of cost for electricity. As the term indicates, it is the average power requirement in KW multiplied by the time in hours over which it is used.

The "single phase circuit" or two-wire system shown in Figure 15 is the simplest circuit. Figure 15 shows a single phase, three-wire system that can furnish two voltages. The three phase (three-wire) is the standard system for large motors. There are two different arrangements of leads from generators or transformers known as delta, Figure 16 and Y shown in Figure 16. Lighting circuits can be taken off as shown. However, unless motors are small, it is better to separate power and lighting circuits to avoid dimming of the lights when motors start.

Circuit protection is provided by fuses enclosed in some type of flame-proof case. They are not always suitable and more complicated thermal relays, air circuit breakers or oil breakers, are required to allow a heavy flow of current for a short time before acting. To allow for a heavy flow, these devices are needed with large motors. A special oil is used in circuit breakers. No other should be used. When a circuit breaker operates frequently, cause should be investigated and corrective steps taken. Protective devices should never be "jumped."

Grounding is extremely important and must be maintained.

Most alternating current "motors" are either of the induction or synchronous type. Synchronous motor speed is determined by the formula,

$N = 120 F/P$ when
N = revolutions of motor per minute (rpm)
F = frequency, cycles per second
P = number of poles
For 60 cycles, $N = 7200/P$

Thus, the fewer the poles, the faster the speed and the smallest possible number of poles is two. Since there must be an even number of poles, the greatest synchronous speed possible for 60 cycles is 3,600 r.p.m. Other possible speeds are 1,800 r.p.m., 1,200 r.p.m., 900 r.p.m., 450 r.p.m. and so forth. The synchronous motor operates accurately at the given speed. This is valuable for clocks and timing devices. However, the synchronous motor has definite poles which must be excited or magnetized by some source of direct current. Synchronous motors have low starting torque (or power), which makes them unsatisfactory for many loads. For this reason it is fortunate that centrifugal pumps can usually be started with small load. Synchronous motors are sometimes used because of their favorable power factor on extremely large pumps.

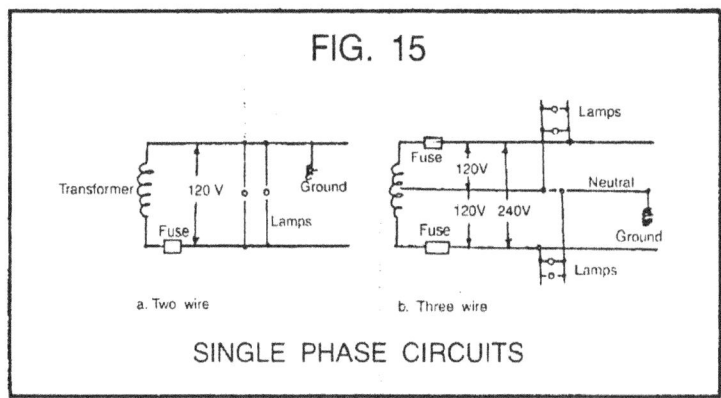

ELECTRIC CIRCUITS

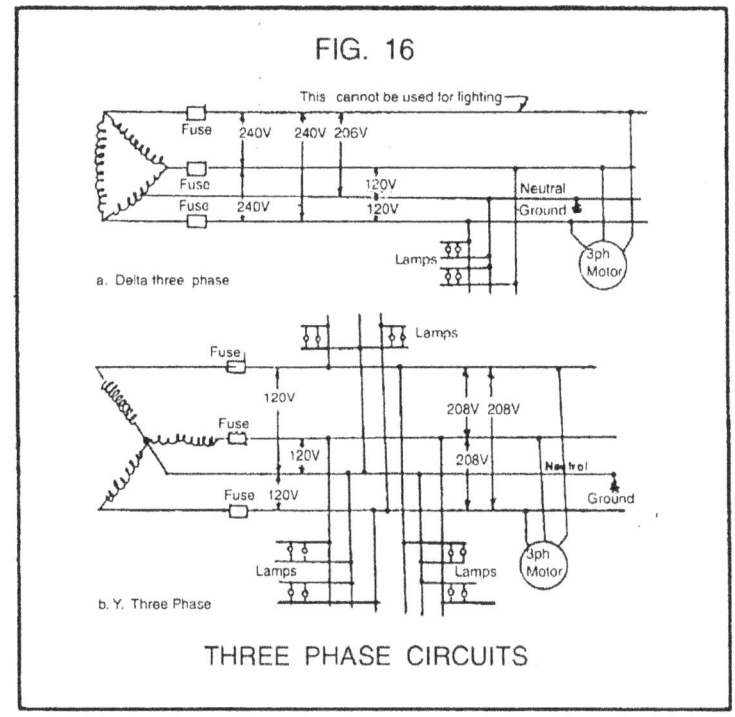

Induction motors. These motors have no poles which need excitation, and can be operated at variable speeds. They are sometimes called squirrel cage motors, because the rotor is made up of bars parallel to the shaft. Without a load, this type of motor will run at a speed close to the synchronous speed. As the load increases, the speed is reduced until at full load the speed is from 2% to 4% less than the synchronous speed. If the load is sufficiently increased, the motor will stop, or "pull out".

Induction motors require relatively small starting currents. Maintenance calls for keeping air ducts and windings of the motor clean. Oil in bearings should be flushed and changed at least once per year. The smaller motors require no special starting devices, and may be started directly across the line. Larger motors usually require reduced voltage for starting.

Variable speed is obtained in an induction motor by having a wound rotor, in whose circuit an external resistance may be added.

Thus a manufacturer can build a motor with external controls to give any speed and power which is required.

"Motor ratings", as well as the ratings for other electrical equipment, are based upon the temperature rise which will occur during operation continuously at normal full load and proper voltage. This rise is usually limited to 40 or 45 degrees centigrade. Thus, a motor may run hot to the touch and still be within its safe rating. A thermometer should be used to check the temperature on small motors. Large motors usually have temperature measuring devices built into them.

ELECTRIC MOTOR AND GENERATOR REPAIR
SELECTION CHARTS FOR MOTORS AND CONTROLLERS

CONTENTS

		Page
TABLE 1.	D.C. Motor Characteristics and Selection Chart	1
TABLE 2.	AC Motor Characteristics and Selection Chart	2
TABLE 3.	Selection Chart for DC Motor Controllers	4
TABLE 4.	Selection Chart for AC Motor Controllers	4

ELECTRIC MOTOR AND GENERATOR REPAIR

SELECTION CHARTS FOR MOTORS AND CONTROLLERS

Table 1. DC Motor Characteristics and Selection Chart

Typical applications		Type of motor	Speed		Starting torque in percent of full load torque	Maximum torque
			Classification	Regulation		

Fans
Blowers
  Positive
  Pressure
 	
Laundry
  Washers
 	
Flat work
  Ironers
 	
Stokers
Dough mixers
	Saws
	  Band
	  Circular
	Joiners
	Molders
	Planners
	
	Line shafts
	Motor-generator
	  sets
	Buffers
	Drill presses
	Grinders
	Lathes
		Shunt-wound	Constant	5 to 10 Percent	150 Percent	Limited by Commutation

Fans Blowers Ironer Flat work Lathe	Boring mill Drills Milling machines Stokers Dough mixers		Adjustable by field control	5 to 15 Percent Dependent upon field setting	150 Percent	
Elevators Passenger Paper mills	Rubber Calendars Mine hoist	Series-wound	Adjustable by variable voltage	Slight	150 Percent	
Cranes Hoists Valves Turntable	Bridges Coal Ore Vehicles		Varying	Dependent upon the load; will run away if unloaded.	300 to 400 Percent	

Pumps
  Centrifugal
  Displacement
Presses
  Printing
  Rotary
 	
Elevators
  Passenger
  Freight
 	
Conveyors
Car pullers
	Crushers
	Large bandsaws
	
	Sanders
	
	Rolls
	  Bending
	  Straightening
	
	Dough mixers
	Laundry
	  Extractors
	Power hammers
		Compound-wound	Varying	10 to 25 Percent	175 to 200 Percent	

Table 2. AC Motor Characteristics and Selection Chart

Applications	Class	Motor Group	Designation	*Starting torque in percent of full load torque	*Starting current in percent of full load torque	Pull-in torque in percent of full load torque	Pull-out torque in percent of full load torque	Slip in percent
Fans Centrifugal Propeller Pumps Centrifugal Rotary Turbine	Squirrel-cage induction—constant speed.	1	Normal torque. Normal starting current.	135 to 200 Percent	Full voltage applied. 500 to 650 Percent. Usually started on reduced voltage.	....	Not less than 200 Percent.	3 to 6 Percent
Joiners Molders Sanders Laundry Washers Job printing		2	Normal torque. Low starting current.	135 to 175 Percent	Full voltage applied 400 to 500 Percent. Meets E.E.I. requirements up to 30 hp. Above 30 hp starting currents may not be within E.E.I. limits.	....	Not less than 200 Percent.	3 to 5 Percent
Positive Pressure Blowers Line shafts Small stokers Metal grinders Planers Pumps Reciprocating Displacement Compressors Air Refrigerating Conveyors Starting Loaded Crushers Without flywheels Bucket-type Elevators		3	High torque. Low starting current.	200 to 250 Percent	E.E.I. limits up to 30 hp 1800 rpm 450 to 550 Percent.	....	Not less than 200 Percent.	5 to 7 Percent
Grain elevator legs Dough mixers Ball mills Large bandsaw Turntables Passenger and freight elevators			High torque.	300 to 400 Percent	300 to 500 Percent	....	Not less than 250 Percent.	12 to 18 Percent
Cranes, hoists, lifts, valves		4	High slip.	Same as for elevators except motor will not meet all conditions as to voltage fluctuations and quiet operation.				

		Application	Motor type					
5		Punch presses, shears, laundry extractors and drives with flywheels or high inertia to accelerate.	High torque. Medium slip.		375 to 500 Percent		300 to 400 Percent	7 to 12 Percent
6	Slipring induction	Drives requiring large starting torques and minimum starting currents, as conveyors, hoist, fans, pumps, compressors, etc. Reduced speed operations of fans, pumps, etc.	Wound rotor induction motor.	Depends on external rotor resistance.			Not less than 200 Percent.	3 to 5 Percent
7	[b] Synchronous	Reciprocating air compressors and other machines which can be started light.	Low speed 100 Percent P.F.[c]	40 Percent	275 to 300 Percent	40 Percent	150 Percent	
8			Low speed 80 Percent P F	40 Percent	250 to 275 Percent	40 Percent	225 Percent	
9		Drives requiring 200 hp or less and 514 rpm or over.	General purpose 100 Percent P F	110 Percent	500 Percent	110 Percent	150 or 175 Percent	
10		Drives requiring 150 hp or less and 514 rpm or over.	General Purpose 80 Percent P F	125 Percent	575 Percent	125 Percent	200 or 250 Percent	

Above values will serve as a guide. [a] Larger values of torque and current apply to the higher speed motors. [b] Synchronous motors are also made to meet other requirements of torque, speed, etc. [c] PF = Power factor. EEI = Edison Electrical Institute.

Table 3. Selection Chart for DC Motor Controllers

Type of motor			Constant speed	Adjustable speed
Method of control			Type of controllers	
For manual control.	Non-reversing	Across-the-line starting (with OL protection).	Manual starters, up to 2 hp. Generally toggle type quick acting with thermal overload.	No
		Reduced current starting (with LV protection).	Rheostat	No
		Speed adjustment (with LV protection).	Rheostat	Rheostat
	Reversing	Across-the-line starting	Drum switch up to 2 hp.	No
		Speed adjustment	Drum controller and armature circuit resistor.	Drum controller and field rheostat.
For magnetic control (remote pushbutton operating)*	Non-reversing	Across-the-line starting (OL and LV protection).	Line starter	No
		Reduced current starting (OL and LV protection).	Time starter	Time starter and field rheostat.
	Reversing	Across-the-line starting (OL and LV protection).	Line starter	No
		Reduced current starting (OL and LV protection).	Time starter	Time starter and field rheostat.

OL = Overload   LV = Low voltage

*Other remote control devices can be used but low voltage release may be obtained instead of low voltage protection.

Table 4. Selection Chart for AC Motor Controllers

Type of motor	For manual control				
	Nonreversing			Reversing	
	Across-the-line starting (with OL protection).	Reduced-voltage starting (with LV protection).	Speed adjustment (with LV protection).	Across-the-line starting.	Speed adjustment.
Squirrel-cage. General purpose. Normal starting torque. Normal starting current.	Manual starter up to 7½ hp. Generally toggle type, quick acting.	(1) Auto-transformer starter with OL protection. (2) Linestarter with OL protection, and primary rheostat.	No	Drum switch up to 15 hp.	No
Squirrel cage. Normal starting torque. Low starting current.	Manual starter up to 7½ hp. Generally toggle type, quick acting.	(1) Auto-transformer starter with OL protection. (2) Linestarter with OL protection, and primary rheostat.	No	Drum switch up to 15 hp.	No
Squirrel-cage. High starting torque. Low starting current.	Manual starter up to 7½ hp. Generally toggle type quick acting.	No	No	Drum switch up to 15 hp.	No
High slip	Manual starter. Generally toggle type, quick acting.	No	No	Drum switch	No
Synchronous	Circuit breaker with field control.	Auto-transformer starter with OL protection and field control.	No	Special	No

Table 4. Selection Chart for AC Motor Controllers—Continued

| Type of motor | For manual control |||||
| | Nonreversing ||| Reversing ||
	Across-the-line starting (with OL protection).	Reduced-voltage starting (with LV protection).	Speed adjustment (with LV protection).	Across-the-line starting.	Speed adjustment.
Wound-rotor or slip-ring.	No	Linestarter for primary control. Rheostat or drum controller for secondary control.	Linestarter for primary control. Rheostat or drum controller for secondary control.	No	Linestarter for primary control. Faceplate, rheostat or drum control for secondary control.
Single phase ½ hp, maximum.	Manual starter. Generally toggle type, quick acting.	Rheostat	No	No	No

OL = Overload.   LV = Low voltage. Drum controller (not switch) include secondary registors.

| Type of motor | For magnetic control (Remote pushbutton operation)* |||||
| | Nonreversing ||| Reversing ||
	Across-the-line starting (with OL and LV protection)	Reduced voltage starting (with OL and LV protection)	Across-the-line starting (with OL and LV protection)	Reduced current starting (with OL and LV protection)
Squirrel-cage. General purpose. Normal starting torque. Normal starting current.	Linestarter	Combination of linestarter and circuit breaker or safety switch.	Resistance-type or auto-transformer starter.	Linestarter	Special
Squirrel-cage. Normal starting torque. Low starting current.	Linestarter	Combination of linestarter and circuit breaker or safety switch.	Resistance-type or auto-transformer starter.	Linestarter	Special
Squirrel-cage. High starting torque. Low starting current.	Linestarter	Combination of linestarter and circuit breaker or safety switch.	No	Linestarter	No
High-slip	Linestarter	Combination of linestarter and circuit breaker or safety switch.	Special	Linestarter	Special
Synchronous	Linestarter with field control.	No	Resistance-type or auto-transformer starter.	Special	Special
Wound-rotor or slip-ring.	Linestarter in combination with secondary controller.	Combination line starter in combination with secondary controller.	Resistance-type starter.	No	Special
Singlephase 7½ hp. maximum.	Linestarter	No	Special	No	No

*Other remote controls can be used but low voltage release may be obtained instead of low voltage protection.

www.ingramcontent.com/pod-product-compliance
Lightning Source LLC
Chambersburg PA
CBHW081824300426
44116CB00014B/2472